In and Out of Love

Dr David Lewis, D.Phil, BSc (Hon), FIDS, is a psychologist, lecturer, broadcaster and the author of many books on psychology. He is a director of Stresswatch, a non-profit-making company which assists people with stress and anxiety problems; he is a founding trustee of Action on Phobias, a charity involved in establishing self-help groups for men and women with phobic difficulties; and he is technical director of Children Unlimited, an organisation which helps parents take a more active role in their children's education. He is author of *The Alpha Plan*, his own specially devised self-help programme for making better use of the brain.

DAVID LEWIS

***

In and Out of Love

***

THE MYSTERY OF
PERSONAL ATTRACTION

A Methuen Paperback

First published in Great Britain 1985
by Constable & Co Ltd as
Loving and Loathing: This Enigma of Personal Attraction
This paperback edition published 1987
by Methuen London Ltd
11 New Fetter Lane, London EC4P 4EE
© 1985 David Lewis
Printed in Great Britain by
Richard Clay Ltd, Bungay, Suffolk

Brititish Library Cataloguing in Publication Data

Lewis, David, *1942–*
    [Loving and loathing]. In and out of love:
    the mystery of personal attraction.
    1. Sex   2. Interpersonal attraction
    Rn: David Lewis Hodgson   I. [Loving and
    loathing]   II. Title
    155.3   HQ21

ISBN 0-413-14510-7

'Carefully Taught' © 1949 Rodgers and Hammerstein II
Used by permission of Williamson Music Limited

'Your Cheatin' Heart' © Acuff-Rose Publications Inc.
Used by permission of Acuff-Music Limited

'Don't All The Girls Get Prettier At Closin' Time'
© 1972 Singletree Music Corporation
Used by permission of Intersong Music Limited

'Jolene' used by kind permission of Carlin Music Corporation
14 New Burlington Street, London W1X 2LR

Extract from 'The Children's Song' from *Puck of Pook's Hill*
by Rudyard Kipling used by permission of The National Trust
for Places of Historic Interest or Natural Beauty
and Macmillan London Ltd

Extract from *Knots* by R. D. Laing
used by permission of Tavistock Publications

Contents

I wish I loved the Human Race;
I wish I loved its silly face;
I wish I liked the way it walks;
I wish I liked the way it talks;
And when I'm introduced to one
I wish I thought What jolly Fun!

Sir Walter Raleigh
Wishes of an Elderly Man

(First wished at a garden-party in June 1914
and endorsed by all right thinking people ever since)

In and Out of Love

1

The enigma of personal attraction

I do not like thee, Doctor Fell,
The reason why I cannot tell;
But this I know, I know full well,
I do not like thee Doctor Fell.

Thomas Brown (1663–1704)

Personal attraction is both a commonplace and a conundrum. Almost daily we decide whether or not we like somebody else, assess the intensity of those feelings and attempt to determine the extent to which they are being returned. Once made, such judgements tend to be remarkably resistant to change and continue exerting a powerful influence over all further dealings with that individual.

Yet while we may have little difficulty in saying whom we like or dislike, look upon as friends or warily regard as foes, it is often extremely difficult, and more than occasionally impossible, to explain the reasoning behind such judgements.

Why are some individuals seen as likeable and others as loathsome, often within moments of our first meeting?

Does it really matter if you are viewed as unattractive, and can those who feel unlovely and unloved do anything about it?

To what extent could the feelings of large groups of people be manipulated to satisfy political ambitions or social goals?

How far can personal attraction be enhanced for one's personal advantage?

It is with possible answers to these important questions that this book is concerned.

We seldom appreciate the extent to which personal attraction shapes our lives and influences our destiny. While it comes as little surprise to discover that such feelings determine our choice of friends and sexual partners, their influence over many other aspects of life, from grades in school to prospects of employment and opportunities for promotion is far less frequently appreciated. Even more remarkable, perhaps, is the effect which attraction can have over such diverse events as the speed of recovery after a physical illness and the effectiveness of therapy for a mental illness, levels of attainment during infancy, and the chances of being elected to political office.

Such feelings may even increase the chances of a jury returning a 'guilty' verdict and the likelihood that, if convicted, a defendant will be imprisoned rather than have a lesser penalty imposed by the judge.

The violent consequences of social, cultural and religious prejudices are well known and daily documented by newspapers and on television. Less easily recognised are the more subtle prejudices aroused by aspects of personality or physique. Often unknowingly, we make important assumptions of other people's outlook and ability on such physical characteristics as body build, skin pigmentation, hair colouring, the size of the nose, the slant of the eyes, and the shape of the face. These beliefs then shape our own collective destiny through their influence over the ways in which, as a nation, we react to social change and national crisis.

The enigma of personal attraction is a matter of everyday experience. Many have had the experience of being physically attracted to somebody while not especially 'liking' them in any other way. Equally we may like a person very much indeed without finding them at all physically attractive. It is perfectly possible to both love and hate another person at virtually the same moment, a paradox finely portrayed – within an adolescent homosexual context, by Robin Cook in his novel, *The Legacy of the Stiff Upper Lip*.

Here the conflict is between the narrator and Greer, a 14-year-old newboy at Eton: 'We hated each other on sight, yet the real tension didn't build up at once; to begin with . . . there were just isolated incidents.'

Greer becomes the victim of the narrator's unceasing verbal and physical aggression. They are isolated: 'Greer had no friends: I prevented him from making any . . .' from the community by mutual loathing. The torture continues, refined and unflagging, until the point is reached where Greer's torture 'now that it had become a secret practised privately between us, redoubled in anguish.'

Finally, after an especially murderous fight, 'as we lolled exhausted on the bed, the inevitable happened and we first had sex together . . . we made love the more passionately for knowing each other so very exactly: predator and victim.'

Greer 'pink and elephantine' was no Adonis, but for the narrator it was this very absence of stereotypic 'good looks' which was such a crucial factor in their mutual physical attraction.

Looks play a vital role in all forms of attraction although it is impossible to define – except within a broad social or cultural context, exactly which aspects of facial form and bodily build will find favour. According to the American humorist, Dorothy Parker, 'Men seldom make passes at girls who wear glasses,' while Anita Loos insisted on the cliché that 'gentlemen prefer blondes'.

When asked about our likes and dislikes we usually produce a shopping list of desirable or undesirable qualities. One person may stress the importance of personality, another place a sense of humour high on their list of valued attributes. Some will say they would prefer a lively, fun loving extravert while others seek the quiet calm of the thoughtful introvert. But, once the list has been drawn up, discussion generally comes to an abrupt halt or goes around in circles. For while we have little difficulty in describing *what* attracts or repels us in another person, it is generally far harder – and often impossible – to say *why* we respond in that way. Like Tom Brown, in his mocking dismissal of the unfortunate John Fell*, feelings about others are far easier to express than to explain.

If pressed we will probably fall back on the explanation that a preference for blondes or brunettes, muscle men or 7-stone weaklings is entirely a matter of personal choice. While this type of circular argument – I like the sort of people I like because those are the type of people I like – may be acceptable in casual conversation it does not advance our understanding of this vitally important aspect of human behaviour.

Before considering what science has to say about the problem of personal attraction, it will be instructive to examine a few of the

* After expelling Tom Brown, Dr John Fell, Dean of Christ Church (1625–86) offered to revoke his order if his student could translate the thirty-third Epigram of Martial: *Non amo te, Zabidi, nec possum dicere quare: Hoc tantum possum dicere non amo te.* The mocking verse was Brown's reply.

ways in which attraction exerts its profound, though seldom fully appreciated, effect.

ATTRACTION IN COURT

Courts of law are generally regarded, if only by those without personal experience of their due processes, as places where all are equal. An image of impartial justice, weighing only the facts of each case before arriving at an objective verdict as to innocence or guilt is firmly established in the public mind.

Reality, as any honest lawyer will confirm, is rather different. Certainly the facts of a case, matters of law as explained by the judge, and the seeming honesty or dishonesty of a defendant's testimony are vital elements in the jury's final verdict.

But there is also the eloquent, but unspoken and rarely acknowledged, testimony of attraction, not only between the defendant and those sitting in judgment on him, or her, but between judge, jury and key witnesses for the prosecution or defence. While being 'attractive' will rarely prove sufficient reason for freeing the obviously guilty, just as being seen as 'unattractive' is seldom going to condemn the clearly innocent, it can prove an important consideration in a very large number of cases in which a 'reasonable doubt' remains.

In their lengthy and detailed research into the workings of the American jury, Harry Kalven and Hans Zeisel of Chicago University cite numerous examples of personal attraction working for or against a defendant. An extreme example was the case of a man charged with the rape of his ten-year-old daughter. At the first trial he was convicted and sentenced to life imprisonment. He appealed and was granted a second trial at which the jury hung. On his third appearance in the dock the jury deliberated for only 30 minutes before returning a *Not Guilty* verdict and presenting the defendant with sixty-eight dollars they had collected among themselves as a mark of their sympathy.

In another case, the judge reported: 'Jury . . . very sympathetic to defendant's wife. Lovely woman, impressed jury. Tears came into wife's eyes on witness stand and four of the jury cried with her.'

Putting together their findings of the various factors which most appealed to a jury, one might suggest that to enjoy the maximum chance of acquittal a defendant should be a good-looking ex-service pensioner with an obvious but not too distressing disability who appears in court smartly but not flashily dressed and, preferably, wearing his medals!

ATTRACTION IN CLASS

Every now and then stories appear in the American and British press, suggesting that in certain universities good-looking students have obtained better grades by having sex with their lecturers. But attraction does not have to take such an obvious form to exert a potent influence on a pupil's educational attainments. From nursery school onwards the likes and dislikes of teachers can serve to create what is virtually a self-fulfilling prophecy of success or failure.

In a study of American kindergarten life, psychologist Dr R. C. Rist of Harvard investigated the extent to which early adult judgements dominate a youngster's whole educational career. In one of the nurseries he investigated, the head teacher placed her young charges on one of three dinner tables according to her expectations of their future academic attainments. Her 'brightest' dined at one table, her 'average' kids on another and her 'failures' ate at a third. When Rist assessed the actual IQs of children on each of the three tables, it was found that the teacher's choice bore no relation to the realities of each child's actual ability.

A bright child could well have been seated at the 'failure' table while less able youngsters could find themselves sitting with her 'intelligent' children. Despite this the teacher saw no reason to promote any child from the 'failure' table or to demote any from the 'success' table. As the years passed, however, the differences in ability between the three groups became more pronounced. Those who had eaten with other 'achievers' did far better, on average, than those who had been condemned to sit with the 'failures'.

Rist commented that the initial prophecy 'came to be justified not in terms of teacher expectations, but in "apparently" objective records of previous school working, including, by the beginning of second grade, reading test performance.' Some might argue that her ability to detect 'bright' and 'dull' children had been triumphantly vindicated. But the truth is that she simply created a self-fulfilling prophecy. The children who had been classed as 'bright' saw themselves that way and were perceived as achievers by influential adults, including parents and other teachers.

The point of interest here is that her original judgements were based largely on how well a child got along with the nursery staff. In other words on the extent to which he, or she, was seen as 'attractive'.

There is no reason to suppose that Rist's findings are exceptional or that similar kinds of bias exist in virtually every educational institution. Why this is very likely to be so will become clear later in the book.

ATTRACTION IN THERAPY

Many psychiatrists and psychologists accept that the YAVIS syndrome plays a significant – if seldom articulated – role in the success or failure of psychotherapy. The acronym, first coined by Dr W. Schofield in 1964, describes the tendency by young male psychiatrists to select for therapy patients who are Young, Attractive, Verbally fluent, Intelligent, Successful, coming from the same social background and having very similar aspirations to themselves. Although Schofield intended the jibe as an ironic comment on one aspect of American psychoanalytic practice, the remark contains more than a grain of truth.

There is an increasing body of research to suggest that the personal relationship between client and therapist is an important factor – some would argue the most important – in the success or failure of many forms of treatment.

Where there is warmth, empathy and mutual regard – in other words a type of attraction that goes beyond the formal boundaries of a professional relationship – positive changes tend to occur more rapidly and to prove more lasting. It is also likely that such 'attraction' exerts a significant influence in physical medicine, with the feelings between doctor and patient, or surgeon and patient playing a role in the speed of recovery and even the levels of pain experienced during treatment.

Yet merely by becoming a 'patient' an individual can, in many cases, reduce the chance of being regarded as 'attractive' by those who treat them. In a recent study of the attitudes of medical students, for example, Dr Jane Santo discovered that they tended to rate 'patients' as much less likeable than 'normals', a judgement based entirely on the sick person's body language.

As will become clear in a moment, a likely explanation for the YAVIS syndrome is the perception of similarity between the individuals concerned. In addition to shared social class and aspirations most psychologists, psychiatrists, doctors and surgeons would regard themselves as being, if not always young and attractive, at least verbally skilled, intelligent and successful.

EXPLORING PERSONAL ATTRACTION

In the past an analysis of personal attraction has been left largely to poets, playwrights, song writers and novelists. It is only fairly recently that scientific interest, especially on the part of psychologists and sociologists, has focused on the topic. Yet, despite widespread and intensive research efforts, it cannot be said that our understanding of the subject has grown much greater. Reports frequently do little more than echo, in scientific language, thoughts that have been expressed by creative artists throughout the ages.

Broadly we can identify two schools of thought in both psychology and in literature. The first claims that similarity is the basis of mutual attraction while the other contends that opposites attract. How might proponents of these contradictory views set about finding evidence in support of their explanation?

Let us look first at the theory of 'attraction through similarity'. In order to identify exactly what it was strangers found attractive about one another, our researchers might adopt a procedure pioneered by the American psychologist Donn Byrne, of Purdue University. His starting point was to ask a number of individuals to fill out a questionnaire which examined their attitudes on such important and controversial issues as unemployment, law and order, abortion, capital punishment, sex before marriage, homosexuality, religious freedom, and nuclear disarmament. At this stage the subjects were not told they were taking part in a study of personal attraction.

A few weeks later the same individuals were invited to the laboratory and asked to help in a project on personality and perception. They were shown questionnaires, apparently completed by two strangers, and asked to form an opinion about the type of person each seemed to be. Finally, they were given a second questionnaire which asked them to rate the same two strangers on a number of personality characteristics and to say how attractive they found each of them.

In fact the completed questionnaires they saw had been filled out by the psychologists based on the information provided by each subject at the earlier assessment. One set of responses closely matched their own views while the other put forward opposing attitudes.

If the 'like attracts like' theory is correct we would expect the subjects to like the person who apparently held similar views better than the one with a very different outlook on life.

Before reviewing the results of this type of study let us look at an alternative experimental approach which sets out to measure the attraction between people who have known one another for some time. Here the usual procedure is to identify a close-knit group – for example students sharing a university hall of residence, people working in the same office, members of the same sporting club and so on. Subjects are asked to complete a questionnaire which investigates the amount of attraction they feel for every other member of the group. In addition, attitudes, personality, or any other feature of interest to a particular investigator are assessed, often through detailed interviews.

What answers have these two approaches come up with? Do

'opposites' attract, or does our liking for others depend on the extent to which they apparently share our beliefs and reflect our views?

In research going back for more than fifteen years, Dr Donn Byrne has consistently found a strong link between attraction and similarity of *opinions and attitudes.* While differences in age, nationality or physical characteristics may influence feelings to some extent, such factors are far less important than sharing an outlook on life. This effect has been found in studies of widely differing groups, from senior citizens to school children, and top management to unskilled labourers. It applies equally to men and to women, to the highly educated and the semi-literate. The message seems clear and unequivocal. If Smith believes Brown holds opinions and attitudes largely similar to his own he will find him attractive. If he thinks Brown holds opposing views he is much less likely to be attracted by him.

At the University of Michigan, Dr Theodore Newcomb followed the developing relationships among a group of male undergraduates from the time they arrived as freshmen, sharing the same dormitory, at Bennington College. They met as strangers, having travelled to Michigan from all over the United States. During the first weeks, as the early, tentative, casual contacts either grew into friendships or withered away, Theodore Newcomb assessed individual attitudes on a wide range of topics and asked each student to state the extent of their like or dislike for all their companions. Like Donn Byrne, he found that students reported greater attraction to those whose attitudes were similar to their own. The firmer a friendship the closer the match between each of those persons' views.

Equally conclusive results were found in a far more dramatic study carried out by W. Griffitt and R. Veitch in 1974. Not content with observing the developing relationships between strangers in a natural setting, these American researchers paid 13 male volunteers to spend ten days in a small ($12' \times 24'$) fall-out shelter. Their surroundings were both hot (86 degrees) and humid (80%) while their diet consisted of 1.25 quarts of water per day, biscuits and sweets. There was only one lavatory, screened by a curtain.

Before entering their shelter, the volunteers completed a 44-item attitude scale. At various times during the experiment they were each asked to indicate which individuals they would like to keep with them in the shelter and which ones they would like to leave the study.

The results were clear. The first two choices of a stranger to be expelled from the shelter were those whose views differed most widely from the volunteer being questioned. The first two choices for those who should remain were those with the highest proportion of similar attitudes.

At first sight, therefore, the case for 'like attracting like' would appear to be firmly established. Birds of a feather do, apparently, 'flock together'. But does sharing another person's attitudes also mean that our personalities are similar and, if so, could this be a further basis for liking?

In an attempt to answer this question, Dr Natalie Reader of the University of Chicago and Dr Horace English of Ohio State University assessed personality and measured degrees of friendship among people who knew one another well. Once again similarity seemed the crucial component. People who rated one another as close friends *were* more like one another on important personality dimensions than was the case for casual acquaintances.

The problem, as you have probably realised, is that this approach has a serious flaw.

If personality tests are given to people *after* they have become friends, one might reasonably argue that each has changed in some way to become more like the other person. They have modified aspects of their personality in order to match the needs of that relationship. For example, an extravert who became friendly with a more introverted individual might experience – and begin to enjoy – some of the quieter pursuits of his companion. Equally the introvert might experiment with lively, more extraverted activities and so develop an outgoing attitude to life.

In an attempt to avoid this difficulty, Dr Carol Izard of Vanderbilt University administered a personality assessment, called the Edwards Personality Profile Sheet, to a group of new students. But, unlike earlier investigators, she did so *before* they arrived at the University. She allowed them six months to get to know one another and then measured attraction in the usual way. The different approach did not, however, produce different results. Like Reader and English she found that those with a similar personality developed the firmest friendships.

Of particular importance were the characteristics of need for achievement, the desire to be self-sufficient and the extent to which an individual sought the company of others.

In summary then, if you are like somebody else in attitudes and personality the chances are you will find them attractive. If you are unlike them you will be less likely to be attracted to that person.

If this was the answer to personal attraction there would be no enigma and the book would end here.

Unfortunately for advocates of what has become known as the

narcissus hypothesis, after the Greek youth who was so handsome he drowned trying to reach his own reflection in a pool, the research findings are not so straightforward as the studies we have described so far suggest.

Donn Byrne, for instance, has established that while shared attitudes appear to form the basis of attraction it is not so much the number of similar views which matters as the *proportion* of similar to dissimilar attitudes. It seems we are willing to allow some points of departure from our own attitudes without the other person appearing any less attractive. Once a critical number has been reached, however, liking rapidly declines. So consistent is this finding that one can express the probability of liking or disliking occurring in terms of the mathematical formula:

$$Y = 5.44X + 6.62.$$

This states that the best way of predicting the extent of a liking response (Y) is to multiply the proportion of similar attitudes (X) by 5.44 and then add 6.62. If, for example, 50% of your views are shared by a colleague the liking response will be 9.34. (i.e. $0.5 \times 5.44 + 6.62$) out of a possible maximum of 12 points. Should you come to accept 80% of one another's views, then liking increases to 10.97.

The discovery that it is the proportion of shared attitudes which really matters could be accommodated within the narcissus theory, by replacing the notion of a exact carbon copy with a slightly fuzzy – though still clearly recognisable replica – of one's attitudes and opinions.

For the many social psychologists who reject the narcissus hypothesis, however, this compromise is as unsatisfactory as the original proposals. By way of explanation they propose a theory which will seem, to many, an even less attractive explanation of personal attraction. Drs Elliott Aronson and Philip Worchel of the University of Texas, for instance, argue that we are attracted to people like ourselves because we assume that similarity of outlook and attitudes make it more likely that the other person *will like us*. In other words, we try to stack the cards in our favour as much as possible in order to reduce the risk of rejection. Clearly, this can best be achieved by concentrating most of our efforts on people who seem as much like us as possible.

Support for this view has come from the researches of Dr George Levinger of Western Reserve University and Dr James Breedlove of Portland State University, who showed that people who are mutually attracted usually believe they have more in common with one another than may actually be the case. In their study, husbands and wives were asked to report their own attitudes as well as those of their spouse on a variety of topics. By comparing the results, Levinger and Breedlove discovered a substantial discrepancy between the opinions which each held and those which their partner *believed* them to hold. They suggested that, in a close relationship, individuals tend to stress similarities of viewpoint in order to conceal or avoid sources of conflict.

If one is to take such findings into account, the apparently straightforward narcissus hypothesis must be expanded to include the fact that we actively seek out those who are most like us in outlook and that, even when such a match is achieved, it may be based on significant misconceptions about what the other person really thinks.

The researches of Professor Raymond Cattell and Dr John Nesselrode of the University of Chicago take us even further from the commonsense notion of 'like attracting like'. In a detailed examination of both happy and unhappy marriages, they administered a personality test, developed by Raymond Catell and known as the 16 PF, to each partner. Computer analysis of the responses revealed the surprising fact that the happiest couples had *opposite* rather than similar personality traits.

Explaining these findings, Raymond Cattell proposed that, when seeking marriage partners, we look for people who show traits of personality which we know we lack but wish we possessed. The traits measured by the 16 PF which predicted marital harmony most successfully were imagination, extraversion, anxiety and what Cattell terms 'ego strength'. This can be defined as the amount of resilience shown in dealing with life's ups and downs. According to these results we might conclude that the most stable and satisfying marriages are those in which, for example, one partner is creative and the other fairly unimaginative, or one is calm while the other is somewhat more anxious, where one is socially inadequate while the other has the ability to get along well with others.

Support for this idea has come from the work of Dr Robert Winch of Northwestern University who concluded that a successful relationship depended on a match between a high level of dominance in one partner and a high level of submissiveness in the other. Winch considers that this applies not only to marriages but to all types of close relationship. He believes that whether we are looking for a friend or a lover our true quest is for someone to complement ourselves.

It is clear that conflicts between the 'like attracts like' and the 'opposites attract' explanations have been heightened rather than resolved by psychological research.

If we are attracted to somebody in proportion to the extent that they mirror important aspects of our own personality and outlook, how can they simultaneously possess diametrically opposite views and attitudes? To understand how differences between these seemingly intractable theories can be resolved one must explore the ways in which we see ourselves in everyday life. You might like to do this for yourself by writing down three headings – / Real Self / Other Self and / Ideal Self / – on a piece of paper.

Under the heading *Real Self* note down all your abilities and aptitudes – both favourable and unfavourable – as they appear to you. This list might, for example, include comments such as: friendly; inclined to be bossy; generous; witty; sarcastic; outgoing; anxious; talkative and so on. Beneath the second heading, *Other Self* you should record the ways in which you feel other people regard you. Included here might be terms such as: impulsive; dominant; reliable; friendly; honest; and aggressive. Finally, under the heading *Ideal Self*, write down all those attributes which you feel you lack but would greatly like to possess, for instance: generousness; assertiveness; understanding; sympathy and an ability to love.

The Ideal Self has been described by Dr R. B. Burns of the University of Bradford as embodying our 'most personal wants and aspirations, part wish and part ought'.

According to Gordon Allport, Emeritus Professor of Psychology at Harvard, our Ideal Self serves as a kind of beacon which helps to pin-point goals in life. He comments that: 'Every mature personality may be said to travel towards a port of destination, selected in advance, or to several ports in succession, their ideal always serving to hold the course in view.'

Real Self and Ideal Self may be very similar to, or vastly different from, one another. It is far from rare to find people with ideas about their Ideal Self which seem to have little in common with the reality of their lives. The result is often unhappiness so great that the individual is finally obliged to attempt a reconciliation between these discrepant self-images. Clearly, there are two main methods by which this gulf can be bridged. First through a change in behaviour which brings about a better match between the Ideal and the actual. Secondly, by altering the Ideal Image so that its goals are more easily achieved. By becoming, for instance, less perfectionist and more pragmatic. By ceasing to strive after the unobtainable. Dr Karen Horney, a founder of the American Institute for Psychoanalysis, believes that the abandonment of this striving for an unrealistic Ideal Self brings about 'one of the great reliefs of therapy'.

If you compile your list thoughtfully, you will probably come up with a rather wide range of perceived abilities, personality attributes, strengths and weaknesses.

Such an exercise is both interesting and, in the context of this discussion, fruitful since it is within such clusters of beliefs that we discover the common ground between those two apparently antagonistic theories. At the University of Chicago, Drs William Thompson and Rhoda Nishimura, designed an experiment to explore the relationship between attraction and the concepts of Ideal and Real Self.

After assessing their subjects on these two components of self-image, they asked them to rate their friends in terms of personality and temperament. The results showed that the majority of subjects regarded their friends as possessing, to a far greater extent than themselves, those qualities listed under the heading of Ideal Self. For example an individual whose Ideal Self included being 'socially confident; assertive; capable and decisive' was most likely to feel attraction for an individual who displayed these qualities. Having discovered such an 'ideal' he soon came to believe that this person possessed those qualities to a considerable extent.

By focusing on the Ideal Self, Thompson and Nishimura identified a factor of central importance to the understanding of personal attraction. For they highlighted a third way in which a gulf between Ideal and Real Self may be bridged. It's often very hard to alter one's behaviour sufficiently to match the demands of Ideal Self, and most of us find it even more difficult to change our ideals. The only remaining option, therefore, is to find a third party to provide the missing link between the ideals and the realities of our lives.

In other words, we find many people psychologically, as opposed to merely physically, attractive in terms of their ability to act out 'roles' in life that we would like to perform but, rightly or wrongly, see as beyond our ability to accomplish. By forming an attachment, which may be close and personal or remote and unrequited, we are able to satisfy, if only vicariously, goals of the Ideal Self. Such people may be close friends or lovers; Royalty or political leaders; industrialists or Union leaders; pop stars, sports stars, film, stage or TV stars. They may be religious teachers or mystics; philosophers or painters; soldiers or scientists. They may even be mass murderers, terrorists or torturers, for no matter how ugly their deeds, somebody, somewhere is almost certain to see them as essential components of the Ideal Self. There are, after all still statues to Stalin in Albania, and shrines at which neo-Nazi faithfuls continue to revere the memory of Adolf Hitler.

By forming such attachments, Real and Ideal selves are reconciled and emotional distress either reduced or removed entirely. Knowingly and willingly or unknowingly and unwittingly these others are woven into the fabric of our psychological being, to perform the role of a surrogate self.

Such a theory helps to explain, for example, why leaders perceived as being weak – no matter how worthy their motives – are generally despised, while those regarded as being 'strong' are widely venerated, no matter how despicable the consequences of their behaviour.

Many people regard themselves as weaker, less in control and less confident than they would like to be and so seek out strength, control and confidence from those in authority.

At least part of the answer to the riddle of loving and loathing may, therefore, lie in the widespread and deeply felt human need not merely to praise famous men but to possess them.

2

Faces and fortunes

There is a Lady sweet and kind,
Was never face so pleased my mind;
I did but see her passing by,
And yet I love her till I die.

Anon (17th century)

The actress Mrs Patrick Campbell is said to have proposed marriage to Bernard Shaw in the belief that any child possessing her beauty and his brains would be doubly blessed.

'Reflect for a moment Madam on the fate of that unfortunate infant,' cautioned the playwright, 'should, by mischance, he be born with your brains and my looks.'

Shaw had a point. When it comes to personal attraction there can be no doubt that appearance plays a crucial role in determining whether a brief encounter will ever develop into a lasting relationship. Whether, in the words of psychologist George Levinger, initial 'awareness' ever warms into intimate 'mutuality'.

We not only react positively or negatively to one another on the basis of a vast range of physical characteristics, from body build to bow legs and from eye-colouring to hair length, but also make important judgements about personality, opinions, attitudes and even IQ's purely from the way the other person looks.

One has only to flick through the old photographs in fashion and film fan magazines to appreciate how swiftly notions of what it takes to be handsome or beautiful change.

The sad truth is that many famed for their looks in the 'Twenties or 'Thirties are likely to appear more laughable than lovely to later generations. Yet despite the ephemeral nature of 'looks' it is still possible to obtain a consensus, with specific time and culture, of what is meant by physical beauty. Once established, that norm becomes established as the goal towards which all must aim in order to enjoy social success and sexual fulfilment.

Such beliefs are, of course, encouraged by the advertising and cosmetics industry, who spend millions of pounds every year persuading people that attraction depends on avoiding spots, not being overweight, possessing broad shoulders or firm breasts, having snow white teeth, no wrinkles and body odours nature never intended.

While almost everybody protests that it is neither fair nor reasonable that people should be judged by appearances, in practice this is what almost always happens. Several studies have confirmed that factors such as intelligence and personality are irrelevant in predicting the degree of liking between young men and women meeting one another socially for the first time – all that matters is the amount of physical attraction. When shown photographs of good-looking strangers most people assume them to be rich and successful, to have high status, a happy marriage, warm personalities, a good social life and sexual potency.

Pictures of 'ugly' people, on the other hand, are associated with concepts of wickedness and evil – however good and kind they may be.

During the 'Sixties The Munsters, a long running and popular American TV show was based entirely on such assumptions. Herman Munster and his family are a collection of Frankenstein grotesques whose mere appearance is supposedly so horrifying that 'normal' men and women jump out of buildings to avoid confrontations with them. The core of humour in the shows came entirely from the paradox of making Herman and his family daunting to look at but fun to know. These stereotyped views are not mere prejudice, however, since they do have some basis in fact.

A recent study of adolescent males, by the American sociologist Robert Agnew, of Emory University, indicated that some delinquents may act ugly because they look ugly. He found that boys rated 'fair' or 'poor' on appearance were more likely to behave antisocially than those rated 'excellent' for looks. Agnew reports that such features as poor complexions, a weight problem or lack of physical maturity can lead others to judge youths as 'more aggressive and less intelligent. They are liked less, and their work is more likely to be judged inferior. They are cut off from society to a certain extent, so they have less to lose by indulging in delinquency'. He cautions that these findings are preliminary and that more work – including a study of girls – needs to be done. But certainly one implication of his conclusions – that attractive youngsters will fare better than unattractive ones – is supported by a large quantity of research evidence.

Numerous studies have shown that good-looking children possess above average self-esteem; handsome or beautiful adolescents date more frequently, experience less anxiety in these encounters and tend to be more sexually experienced, while attractive adults are more likely to be successful – personally and professionally – in life.

Clearly then, much of what we know, or assume, about another person comes not from what they say but from what their face and body tell us. Attraction is conveyed through a multitude of non-verbal messages: stature and body shape, facial features, skin and hair pigmentation, eye coloration, posture, expression, gesture and gaze.

Within *four minutes* of the first meeting, according to American psychiatrist Leonard Zunin, people decide whether they will remain strangers or develop warm friendships.

When making up our minds we depend, to varying degrees, on stereotyped assumptions about the link between body language and behaviour. Plump 'endomorphs' are expected to be jolly, affable, tolerant, sociable and calm while lean 'ectomorphs' are viewed as tense, cautious, and precise.

Red-heads are regarded as hot-tempered; people with glasses are believed to have above average intelligence; long hair is associated with liberal attitudes on such issues as capital punishment and drug-taking; men with flowing white beards are looked upon as wise; blondes are supposed to be dumb; while tall men are generally seen as being more powerful and sexually attractive to women than shorter males. What gypsy fortune-teller ever told a client she was going to meet a *short* dark stranger!

In the eighteenth century popular prejudices dating back to antiquity – Aristotle wrote on the importance of studying the face in order to assess temperament – achieved the status of a 'science' when the Swiss theologian, Jonathan Kaspar Lavater, created a precise measuring technique and an exact set of rules for deducing personality from physical appearance. Using his procedures, assessments were made on the basis of such characteristics as nose size, distance between the eyes, and chin shape.

It was not until the nineteenth century, however, that this fascination with measuring various features of a person's skull in order to determine personality and intellectual capacity found its apotheosis in the heyday of the pseudoscientific pursuit of craniology. Francis Galton, eminent cousin of Charles Darwin and a pioneer of modern statistics, was a passionate believer in the value of measurement for scientifically assessing degrees of human attractiveness. He even constructed a 'beauty map' of Britain by means of an elaborate, and entirely idiosyncratic assessment procedure: 'Whenever I have the occasion to classify the persons I meet into three classes, good, medium and bad', I use a needle mounted as a pricker, wherewith to prick holes, unseen, in a piece of paper torn rudely into a cross with a long leg. I use its upper end for 'good', the cross arm for 'medium', the lower end for 'bad'. The prick holes keep distinct, and are easily read off at leisure . . . I use this plan for my beauty data, classifying the girls I passed in streets or elsewhere as attractive, indifferent or repellent. Of course this was a purely individual estimate, but it was consistent, judging from the conformity of different attempts in the same population. I found London to rank the highest for beauty; Aberdeen lowest.'

In 1884, Galton opened a laboratory at the International Exposition in London where he tested and measured any member of the public prepared to pay 3 pence for the privilege. When the Exposition ended, Galton maintained his testing centre at a London museum for a further six years.

All this might have been little more than a harmless Victorian eccentricity, had there not been a far darker and more dangerous side to such assessments. Skull size, as a measure of brain size, and the shape of the head – especially the angle of the jaw – rapidly became powerful weapons in the cause of racial prejudice, so providing judgement by stereotype with a seemingly scientific rationale.

At the forefront of this work was Anders Retzius, a Swedish scientist, and his 'cranial index', a technique for classifying head shapes from the ratio of maximum width to maximum length. Long skulls* he termed dolichocephalic, while skulls with a relatively short ratio, were called brachycephalic. Upon this simple, not to say simple-minded, measure Retzius founded a theory of civilisation.

According to his view, the primitive Stone Age population of

---

* Technically, dolichocephalic skulls had a ratio of 0.75 or less, while brachycephalic skulls had a ratio of 0.8 or more.

Europe were brachycephalic while the more advanced Bronze Age peoples, the forebears of Aryan, or Indo-European, peoples were dolichocephalics. Survivors of the original brachycephalic stocks could still be discovered, Retzius believed, among the Lapps, Basques and Finns. Although disputed by many leading scientists, including the eminent French surgeon Paul Broca, the cranial index and – especially – the notion of links between skull shape and intelligence were widely believed and extremely influential.

From this work stemmed Cesare Lombroso's concept of 'criminal man', a theory which the Harvard anthropologist Steven Jay Gould describes as 'probably the most influential doctrine ever to emerge from the anthropometric tradition'.

In 1870 this Italian physician had been attempting without much success to identify anatomical differences between criminals and the insane. Then, on a gloomy morning in December, while examining the skull of a brigand named Vihella he suddenly 'saw' in the cranial structure evidence of an apish past.

'It was not merely an idea, but a flash of inspiration,' he later wrote. 'I seemed to see all of a sudden, lighted up as a vast plain under a flaming sky, the problem of the nature of the criminal – an atavistic being who reproduces in his person the ferocious instincts of primitive humanity and the inferior animals.

'Thus were explained anatomically the enormous jaw, high cheekbones, prominent superciliary arches, solitary lines in the palms, extreme size of the orbis, handle-shape ears found in criminals, savages and apes, insensibility to pain, extremely acute sight, tattooing, excessive idleness, love of orgies, and the irresponsible craving for evil for its own sake, the desire not only to extinguish life in the victim, but to mutilate the corpse, tear its flesh and drink its blood'.

From this view of anatomy as destiny, Lombroso proceeded to compare criminals with groups of human beings designated – on the basis of body size, head shape and other characteristics – as being 'inferior'.

Others quickly followed his lead. The sexologist Havelock Ellis was much impressed by the 'fact' that both criminals and 'inferior' races are incapable of blushing. He remarked that an 'Inability to blush has always been considered the accompaniment of crime and shamelessness. Blushing is also very rare among idiots and savages'.

The French sociologist Gabriel Tarde, a professor of philosophy and an official of the Ministry of Justice, expressed the view that some European criminals 'would have been the ornament and moral aristocrats of a tribe of Red Indians'.

In England, Dr John Langdon Haydon Down, Medical Superintendent at Earlswood Asylum for Idiots* argued that the features of lower races could be discovered in mentally subnormal children. Dr Down claimed to have identified idiots of the 'Ethiopian variety' who were 'white negroes, although of European descent' and others of Malay or, especially, Mongolian stock: 'A very large number of congenital idiots are typical Mongols,' he wrote in 1866. Describing one young patient he remarked that it was difficult to realise the boy had European parents, but concluded that: 'So frequently are these characters presented, that there can be no doubt that these ethnic features are the result of degeneration.'

These eccentric ethnic views are today recalled by still widespread, if fortunately decreasing, use of the word 'mongol' to describe children suffering from a form of mental deficiency. The correct clinical term, Down's syndrome, enshrines the doctor's name while ignoring his prejudices.

So far as Lombroso was concerned, if any non-European races existed in whom the Italian criminologist could discover the slightest vestige of decency he failed to write about them.

He described the noses of the Dinka tribe in the Upper Nile as resembling those of a monkey and believed that gypsies: 'have the improvidence of the savage and that of the criminal as well . . . they are given to orgies . . . they murder in cold blood in order to rob and were formerly suspected of cannibalism'. He also cited an insensitivity to pain among negroes and 'American savages' as clear evidence of the atavistic inheritance. 'The former cut their hands and laugh in order to avoid work; the latter, tied to the torture post, gaily sing the praises of their tribe while they are slowly burnt.'

At times other features of the human body became the focus of interest for Lombroso's followers. In 1896, for example, delegates to the 4th International Congress of Criminal Anthropology were given an illustrated lecture on the subject of prostitutes' feet by one L. Jullien. Commenting on his illustrations, Lombroso remarked that they showed 'admirably that the morphology of the prostitute is more abnormal even than that of the criminal, especially for atavistic anomalies, because the prehensile foot is atavistic'.

'His thoughts revolutionized our opinions, provoked a salutary feeling everywhere, and a happy emulation in research of all kinds,' wrote Dallemagne, an eminent opponent of Lombroso's views. 'For 20 years, his thoughts fed discussions . . . his thoughts appeared as events. There was an extraordinary animation everywhere.'

However extreme and pseudoscientific Lombroso's views may

---

* This was a technical term used in the British Mental Deficiency Act (1927) to define a grade of mental defective.

appear today, less than a century since Dallemagne wrote those words, their influence over the legal and penal argument of the time were considerable and remained so for many years after his death in 1909.

Every four years, right up to the start of the First World War, the latest 'research' findings, derived from Lombroso's ideas, were debated at an international conference attended by eminent scientists, judges, jurists and government officials, from many parts of the world.

In 1921 Ernst Kretschmer, a German psychiatrist, published *Physique and Character* (*Korperbau und Charakter*) in which he extended Lombroso's theory of personality based on skull types to one involving measurement of the whole body. Kretschmer claimed to have identified three character types which matched, although in a much reduced form, the mental illnesses from which they were derived. The schizophrenic mentality corresponded to a bodily type he named 'leptosomic'. These people were slender with small shoulders, thin arms, fine hands and a long, small, flat chest.

People whose illness was characterised by sudden mood changes, such as manic depression, were 'Pyknics', characterized by being medium-sized and squat, with a barrel chest extending into a portly paunch. Their soft, broad faces are supported by a massive neck, while their noses are wide, flat, and fleshy.

Finally there was the 'Barykinetic' category, with an athletic body build: a solid, high set head, thick skin, abundant hair and robust, muscular body. They were characterised temperamentally by their tendency to repress emotions to the point where they burst forth in explosive violence.

'The formula of an individual's constitution is packed into his facial structure,' Kretschmer wrote. 'And over this indirect course the anatomical structure of the face becomes an index of his spiritual nature . . .'

William H. Sheldon, an American physician, followed Kretschmer's lead by seeking a link between physique and temperament among university students. After developing a seven-point rating scale for measuring bodily characteristics (somatypes), Sheldon proceeded to photograph 46,000 young American males in the nude – in the 'Forties when he began his work it was considered improper to include females in the study. Each photograph was then rated on a seven-point scale before that individual's personality was assessed.

Using this technique he found 88 different kinds of physique ranging from extreme endomorphs, a male 5′ 10″ tall and weighing

200 lbs would come into this category, through the muscle-man mesomorph (weighing in at around 175 lbs for the same height), to extreme ectomorphs (weighing 100 lbs for the same height).

Scoring was carried out by first rating the body on endomorphy, then on mesomorphy and, finally, on ectomorphy. Different parts were assessed separately – legs, shoulder, chest and so on – on each of the three scales and an average taken. This could give a high-endo subject a final rating of, say, 631 while a person with a high-meso score might be rated 262. Sheldon's average value for American males – based on 46,000 subjects – was 343. Later researchers have scaled professional boxers at 262; women Olympic swimmers at 552 and top fashion models at 245.

Sheldon further claimed to have found an association between paunchy endomorphs and a relaxed, sociable approach to life. Muscular mesomorphs, by comparison, were more likely to be energetic, assertive and courageous, while tall, slender, ecto-morphs tended to possess restrained, introverted personalities and creative intellects.

A major criticism of his work is that those rating the photographs are likely to have brought to their task stereotyped ideas about the way plump, muscular and thin people are most likely to behave. A stout student, for instance, might be judged as 'jolly' and a thin one 'sensitive' no matter how they actually behaved. Despite these and other serious flaws in Sheldon's research, it proved influential and contributed towards the present conviction that character can be read from facial features and body shape.

In his book *Reading Faces*, Dr Leopold Bellak, a psychology professor at New York University and psychiatry professor at Albert Einstein Medical College, provides a detailed and compre-hensive method – the Zone System – for personality assessment based on an analysis of facial features.

'Although one's face is influenced primarily by genetic factors, experience alters one's facial features considerably,' he says. 'Changes take place in the underlying bone and muscle structure and are modified through the repetition of emotional response.' Bellak's key to interpreting character from faces is a 101 Traits Checklist consisting of adjectives which describe both physical and emotional characteristics.

To illustrate his Zone System in action, Professor Bellak carried out an analysis of Da Vinci's enigmatic masterpiece the Mona Lisa. The first step was to divide the portrait down the middle so delin-eating the left and right sides. With the left side of La Gioconda's face covered, the expression became, according to Professor Bellak, 'subtly sardonic, perhaps even disdainful. The right half of her mouth is set tight. As a psychiatrist, I interpret that tightness as controlled sensuality.' By covering the right zone he discovered a left eye which is 'slightly pensive, almost squinting. The left half of her mouth is relaxed, softened in the semblance of a smile.'

Repeating the process horizontally, Bellak pinpointed such features as bulging lower eyelids, adding intensity to her smile and full, round cheeks which convey an air of sensual pleasure.

'In the Mona Lisa, the suggestion of sensual indulgence by the cheeks, and the implication of a lack of stricture by the weak chin, add up to a lot of promise to the roving male eye.'

Bellak has also analysed the faces of the more recently famous seeing in a newspaper portrait of Marilyn Monroe, sadness, perplexity, pain and introspection.

'She seems vulnerable and lost,' he says, explaining how her right zone carries the suggestion of a smile around the eyes which indicates a sense of humour and is more calmly self-possessed than the left side of the face. 'Her eyes are inner-directed and contemplative. Her nose is firm with tight nostrils, suggesting an effort at self-control.' In the lower zone he finds a 'surprisingly tight' mouth and a firm jaw – features which conflict with the softly sensuous lips and mouth seen in so many of the star's film roles.

Bellak claims that this form of analysis has proved a clinically valuable diagnostic tool.

But, as with Sheldon's work, a serious criticism is that judgements about the character of those being analysed are likely to be seriously affected both by stereotyped views and by any knowledge of the subject which the viewer brings to that task. It is widely known, for example, that Marilyn Monroe had an unhappy childhood and went though several failed marriages before her death from a drug overdose.

But how accurately can people assess character from the facial features of men and women known only from their photographs? Under these conditions the only likely influence will come from stereotyped attitudes towards different physical attributes. Such an investigation has been carried out by Dr Rudolf Cohen of the University of Konstanz in West Germany.

In an extensive and carefully controlled experimental study ranging over several years, Dr Cohen first gave a battery of standard psychological tests to a large number of volunteers. They assessed subjects on such traits as extraversion, introversion and neuroticism. He also measured social attributes like popularity and dominance.

Each subject was then photographed and the pictures shown to a second group of volunteers – strangers to the first – who were asked to make personality judgements and to provide a list of the key features, such as width of face, shape of nose, prominence of mouth, height of hairline and size of ears, which led them to those conclusions. Computer analysis of the data showed that the results obtained were no better than chance. Not only was it impossible to discover any link between the judgements and the subject's actual personality, but features allegedly indicating a particular trait varied considerably from one viewer to the next. Some people claimed, for example, that the 'distance of eyebrow to eye' was a sure sign of a lively, extravert personality, while others regarded exactly the same feature as a clear indication of introversion.

A further investigation, in which facial characteristics were compared with the measured personality of each individual, revealed an equally random distribution. When a specific feature corresponded with a particular personality trait then it was purely a matter of luck. The significant point, therefore, is not that thick lips indicate a sensual nature or a broad forehead reveals a high level of intellect, but that many people *believe* they do.

When asked about the importance of such influences in their liking or disliking, however, most people attempt to play down – or deny entirely – their significance. 'It's not looks that count but the kind of person you are that matters,' they insist.

All the evidence, however, refutes this assumption. Indeed, the tendency to view good-looking individuals more favourably starts very early on in life, as a study by Drs Dion and Berschied of Winconsin University clearly showed. Karen Dion and Ellen Berschied asked groups of 4–6 year olds in kindergartens to say which of their classmates they liked the best and the least. Even at this age physically attractive boys and girls received more votes than their less good-looking companions. As the children grow older this bias is strengthened and markedly affects a wide range of judgements.

In a paper entitled 'Beauty is Talent' Drs David Landy and Harold Sigall of the University of Rochester explored one aspect of this bias – its role in influencing the assessment of intellectual ability.

A group of male undergraduates were asked to read an essay, supposedly written by a female student at the same university, and then rate both the work itself and the writer's ability in several areas of academic importance. Attached to some of the essays, as if in error, was a photograph of the supposed author – it had, in fact, been written by Landy and Sigall themselves.

Two versions of the essay were prepared, one being well and the other poorly written. Some of the subjects received either a good or poor quality essay and a photograph of an attractive girl, others were given one of the two versions accompanied by the picture of a less attractive girl while the remainder were handed either a good or bad essay without any snapshot.

As might be expected the students who read a good essay rated the writer and her work more highly than those who were handed a bad one, which showed that they were perfectly capable of distinguishing between high and low quality work. However, within these groups there was a significant tendency for the students to rate both the writer and her work more highly if she was considered attractive and less highly when she was regarded as unattractive. Essays without any picture generally received an intermediate rating. The bias was most pronounced when the essay was poorly written. This study raises several disturbing questions as it suggests that even people who are quite capable of telling good work from bad may be misguidedly influenced by another's looks.

Nor can the conclusions be ducked by assuming that trained teachers would be far less open to such an influence than fairly naïve undergraduates. When a somewhat similar experiment was performed using professional teachers as subjects much the same outcome was obtained. Dr Walter Berger of the University of Augsburg in Germany asked secondary school teachers to state their expectancies about certain students. An analysis of the results shows that the more attractive the child the higher a teacher's expectations.

In a related study Walter Berger and Heinz Schuler decided to investigate the extent to which looks affected the prospect of obtaining employment. The two researchers gave fake job application forms, together with a photograph of the supposed applicant, to 80 personnel managers and asked them not only to rate that individual's chances of being short-listed but to comment on several other aspects of job success. Not only did the attractive applicants stand a far better chance of being offered an interview, they were also rated more highly on such positive attributes as friendliness, creativity and motivation.

Psychologist Dr Karen Dion, whose researches I have already described, also studied this type of bias with similar results. She found that good-looking men and women were expected to be more successful in both their private and professional lives than those who were less obviously attractive. Furthermore Dr Dion's subjects automatically attributed several socially desirable qualities to attractive strangers, yet assumed that ugly ones must lack these attributes.

The fact that attractive people *are* more likely to do well in their professional lives is a tribute to the potency of these otherwise quite unjustified and unjustifiable conclusions.

The practical consequences of this need to be seen as attractive can be seen at their most dramatic in Japan where intense competition for jobs has led many graduates to fear that their degrees alone will not prove an adequate passport to a worthwhile career. In the not unreasonable hope that their face will be their fortune many visit plastic surgeons before starting the round of interviews. One specialist hospital reported that in 1982 alone 5,000 students had cosmetic surgery carried out – a figure which is expected to double by 1984. The deputy director commented that students now accounted for 45% of the hospital's patients compared with only 15% in 1972. Although employers deny that looks are important, students who are prepared to invest up to 400,000 yen (£1,150) reveal a better understanding of the psychology of interviewing. They know that when it comes to finding employment good looks count for more than good grades.

Yet physically attractive people do not have everything going for them. Studies suggest that mesomorphs, so prized by Sheldon, may be sightly more vulnerable to heart attacks than other body types while research by a group of American psychologists showed that good looks do not make people especially memorable.

Leah Light, of Pitzer College, Claremont, Steven Hollander and Fortunee Kayra-Stuart of the Clarement Graduate School used photographs in high-school year-books to assess the impact of looks on memory. 120 pictures of white, male graduate seniors were shown to a panel of volunteers who were asked to rate those pictured on a 5-point scale of 'usualness', ranging from 1 (very usual) to 5 (very unusual).

A separate group of white male students at the University of California's Los Angeles campus then rated the same pictures on a 7-point scale from 'least good-looking' to 'very good-looking'. Finally the researchers assessed each face's 'memorability' by flashing slides of the photographs on to a screen and later giving their subjects a paper-and-pencil memory test.

The results were clear. Individuals rated as most typical or ordinary are also judged most attractive but their faces prove the hardest to remember. It was the 'unattractive' and atypical faces that could most easily be linked to a name.

This study provides an important clue to the nature of physical attraction by highlighting the fact that it is a lack of distinguishing features that forms an important component of good looks.

The finding is not new, however. Francis Galton explored the nature of ordinariness in features by the novel method of creating composite photographs in which the features of several people were superimposed to create a single print. The results appealed to most people as 'a very striking face, thoroughly ideal and artistic, and singularly beautiful'.

In a series of experiments using different photographs, Galton was repeatedly impressed by 'how beautiful all composites are. Individual peculiarities are all irregularities, and the composite is always regular'.

But attraction, like all forms of communication, is a two-way process. Clearly our views on what constitutes beauty will be influenced by social fashions and cultural traditions. But more personal factors – including our needs – play an equally crucial part in determining just how attractive we find another person.

The truisms of folk psychology, which have often found scientific support in the laboratory, can sometimes be gleaned from the lyrics of popular songs.

Dr James Pennebaker of the University of Virginia Psychology Department was intrigued by a comment Country and Western song-writer Baker Knight included in a hit number: / 'Ain't it funny, ain't it strange, / the way a man's opinions change / When he starts to face that lonely night.' Deciding that the song – 'Don't All the Girls Get Prettier at Closin' Time' – advanced a testable hypothesis, James Pennebaker decided to take his researches out of the laboratory and into the bars. Research assistants of both sexes visited local bars at 9.30 pm, 10.30 pm and 12.30 pm – immediately before closing-time. They selected as subjects men and women who were alone and appeared 'fairly sober'. A researcher of the same sex approached the chosen individual and asked whether he, or she, would be prepared to take part in an experiment. All 103 people asked agreed to co-operate.

Adopting an approach suggested by the lyric 'If I could rate them on a scale of 1 to 10, looking for a 9 but 8 could fit right in . . .', the researchers asked their subjects to do just that to members of the opposite sex patronising the bar. The results provided strong support for Baker Knight's lyrical suggestion. As closing-time gets closer people left without partners start to see members of the opposite sex as increasingly attractive.

Pennebaker offers two explanations for these findings. His first is based on the psychological theory of 'reactance' which states that when our freedom to act or to make a decision is threatened we respond by regarding that option as more and more desirable. Here the possibility of finding a partner for the night comes under increasing threat as time passes. This makes it seem even more desirable and, therefore, the range of people who might serve as satisfactory partners undergoes progressive expansion.

The second explanation is based on an idea called 'cognitive dissonance' first put forward by American psychologist Leon Festinger in 1957. He suggested that motives for human actions arise from a dissonance, or disturbing discrepancy, created when somebody holds two irreconcilable ideas simultaneously. Because dissonance is distressing it stimulates a desire for change.

Suppose, for example, somebody both smokes heavily and reads a great deal about the health dangers this involves. Since believing what you are doing may cause serious damage to your health cannot be reconciled with continuing to smoke, dissonance will be created. At this point, in order to reduce these unpleasant feelings, the heavy smoker must either give up cigarettes or disbelieve the fact that it does much harm. She, or he, may say, 'It's a risk but then most things in life have an element of risk . . .' or else tell you how their Uncle Charlie lived to over 80 while smoking 50 cigarettes a day.

Dissonance arises in the bar when somebody who hopes to pick up an attractive partner finds fewer and fewer people to choose from. In order to reduce these feelings, those remaining will be seen as better and better looking as the night wears on.

But what physical features are those bar room hopefuls on the look-out for? Drs Jerry Wiggins, Nancy Wiggins and Judith Conger, from the University of Illinois, decided to test out the male 'locker-room' folklore that among heterosexual males there are 'leg men', 'breast men' and 'bottom men'.

In their study 95 male subjects were showed silhouettes of nude females and asked to rate them for attraction. During separate sessions the same men completed a range of personality tests.

Although it has been established that women are less influenced by physical appearances than men when it comes to appreciating the opposite sex, a similar study by Dr Sally Beck of Butler University, this time using silhouettes of males, showed that female preference also provides clues about the personality of those who make the choices.

I have adapted findings from both these studies to provide you with a guide to what your own preferences reveal. All you have to do is select those features of the two silhouettes below which seem most attractive and then read my comments under the appropriate heading.

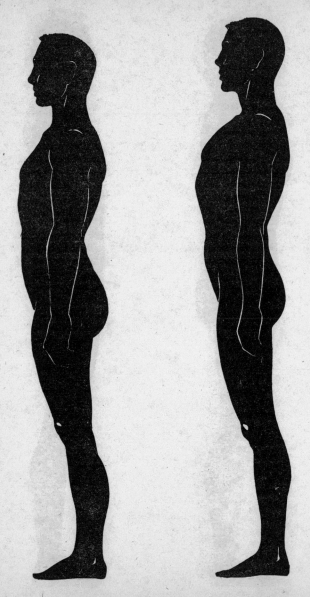

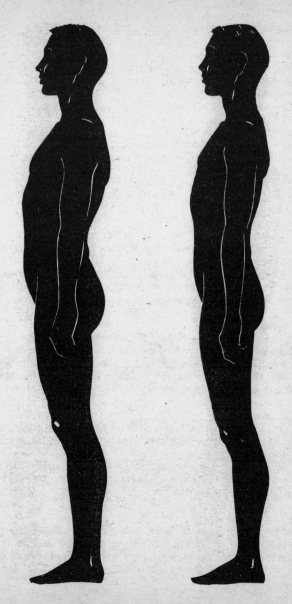

40

Large breasts

Men who prefer large breasts have been found to date frequently,
enjoy typically 'masculine' interests, follow sports and have an
above-average sex drive.

They like showing off, enjoy being the centre of attention, favour
relationships that give a great deal of freedom and dislike having
their independence challenged.

They are more likely to be smokers than non-smokers, tend
towards impatience and find it difficult to persevere in the face of
set-backs.

They seldom worry much, taking each day as it comes, but like
surrounding themselves with material possessions.

Small breasts

Males with a preference for small breasts tend not to drink much
alcohol, suffer bouts of mild depression and prefer warm, empathic
relationships.

Somewhat conformist in their social attitude they have a strong
need for achievement and work hard to make a success of their
careers, persevering despite set-backs and difficulties.

Large buttocks

This choice is related to a desire for order and organisation in life.
Males who favour this part of the anatomy seek out the views of
others before taking decisions and like to have support for their
actions. They are dependent in relationships and tend to blame
themselves when things go wrong.

Small buttocks

This preference indicates an ability to persevere in complex or
demanding tasks and a reluctance to accept the blame when things
go wrong.

They have no desire to be the centre of attention, and are unlikely
to be much interested in sports. As babies they were more likely to
have been breast-fed.

Short legs

A preference for short legs is linked to a liking for the company of
others and for social situations in which it is possible to be the focus
of attention. There is a strong desire to be helpful and a need to feel
wanted, trusted and liked by others.

Long legs
Males who find long legs an attractive feature are usually non-aggressive and blame themselves when things go wrong, even though the mistake was not really their fault. They are deep thinkers and more introspective than most, preferring to live life at a relatively slow pace and showing little interest in business matters. If obliged to choose one parent they would prefer their mother to their father. They are rather inhibited and fairly restrained in social situations.

The 115 female undergraduates who took part in Dr Beck's study overwhelmingly preferred men with small buttocks to large, and although moderately large chests were favoured, there was only a moderate interest in very large ones. The length of a man's legs made absolutely no difference to his attractiveness.

MALE SILHOUETTE – PHYSIQUE FOUND ATTRACTIVE

Large thickset man
Women who prefer this body shape in the male usually enjoy sports and physical activity and regard themselves as less traditionally feminine.

Large chest and small buttocks
This choice is usually made by achievement-orientated women, especially those with academic or professional backgrounds.

Small chest and moderate size body
Women with a more traditional view of the female role were most attracted to this outline.

Thin body
The choice of women from higher social and economic backgrounds.

As can be seen the research suggests a far less specific link between particular parts of the body and traits of personality. In general the physical characteristics women desire in men differ greatly from the masculine stereotype. Of special appeal, according to writer Rosalind Coward is 'sexual surprise', that is, the discovery of female characteristics within an otherwise 'masculine' appearance. These can include, long eye-lashes, pretty faces and soft hair on muscled arms. Slim, trim, rounded but firm male bottoms are also liked – the kind of bottom that could just as easily be seen on a woman.

Disliked features include drooping moustaches, wiry hair pro-
truding from a tightly buttoned denim shirt and bulging muscles.

Yet it is rarely physical attributes alone which appeal to women,
who are more often attracted by what the body symbolises in terms
of power, comfort and protection.

In this chapter I have focused largely on heterosexual attraction, the area in which most research has been done, and posed
questions rather than providing possible answers.

Why should some physical features appeal so much more strongly
that others? If, as some psychologists believe, there is a link
between liking and personality traits what causes them to form?

Later in the book I shall be offering answers to these questions
and looking in slightly more detail at the components of attraction
between members of the same sex and within the family. But before
we can leave bodily features to concentrate on the psychological
aspects of attraction there is one other physical component of
mutual liking that must be taken into account.

It is a factor which has only really come into prominence during
the last few years, but now attracts the attention of researchers in
many parts of the world. Proclaimed by some as a vital element in all
forms of attraction, and dismissed by others as utterly irrelevant to
human liking, it appeals to one of our most powerful, yet usually
least regarded, senses – the sense of smell.

3

Smell of success

Thy baths shall be the juice of July-flowers,
Spirit of roses, and of violets,
The milk of unicorns, and panthers' breath
Gathered in bags, and mixed with Cretan wines.
Our drink shall be prepared gold and amber;
Which we will take, until my roof whirl round
With the vertigo.

Ben Jonson (1573–1637)
Volpone

'Odours act powerfully upon the nervous system,' commented the seventeenth-century writer Johannes Muller. 'They prepare it for all pleasurable sensations, they communicate to it that slight disturbance or commotion which appears as if inseparable from emotions of delight, all which may be accounted for by their exercising a special action upon those organs whence originated the most rapturous pleasure of which our nature is susceptible.'

The importance of smell in attraction was noted by Aristotle, some three centuries before the birth of Christ. Among the Romans aromatic baths were a regular prelude to love-making, as were massages with sweet-smelling unguents and the use of perfumes on the head, body, hair and clothing. Civet and ambergris were especially popular among the wealthy leisured classes of Imperial Rome, with aromatic spices to sweeten the breath. The importance of vanilla as an aphrodisiac can be seen by the fact that the name of this spice is a diminutive of the Latin term *vagina*.

The potency of olfactory stimulation was well-known to Oriental sexologists, especially the Arabs and Jews.

Mohammed wrote of his love for women and perfumes. Ruth anointed herself with fragrant oils. Esther purified herself with the oil of myrrh, Judith with precious ointment.

The Song of Solomon includes the verse:

Awake, O north wind; and come, thou south;
Blow upon my garden, that the spices thereof may flow out.
Let my beloved come into his garden,
And eat his pleasant fruits.

In Proverbs, (7, 17–18) we are told:

I have perfumed my bed with myrrh, aloes and cinnamon. Come, let us take our fill of love until the morning; let us solace ourselves with loves.

When in the sixteenth century Sheika al-Nefzawi of Tunisia wrote one of the world's earliest sex manuals, it was no coincidence that he entitled it *The Perfumed Garden*.

Given this long historical recognition of the important role played by odours in human attraction and sexual arousal, it is perhaps surprising that the serious scientific investigation of smell – olfaction – should be of fairly recent origin. Indeed it is only within the past few decades that the mechanisms by which we smell have been properly understood. Today a major focus of research interest lies in a group of chemicals known as 'pheromones'.

The term, which was only coined in 1959, comes from two Greek words meaning to 'convey' and to 'urge on'. As the name suggests a pheromone is a chemical used for communication between insects and between certain other animals, and can be likened to hormones which provide chemical communication between organs within the body.

Aristotle described how certain butterflies and moths were attracted to one another on the basis of odours, observations which received scientific confirmation in the nineteenth century by the great French naturalist Jean Henri Fabre.

Indeed, the record for the most acute sense of smell in the animal kingdom is held by the male Emperor moth (*Eudia pavonia*) who can detect pheromones from a virgin female nearly seven miles upwind. This feat is even more remarkable when one realises that the odour involved is produced by an alcohol of which only 0.0001 milligrammes is present in the female's body.

The same effect can be seen in other types of insects. Male

silkworms, for example, are drawn irresistibly to females of the same species by a pheromone called *bombykol*. So powerful is its effect that males will attempt to copulate with any object, even a small piece of paper, which has been treated with the substance.

It is not only sexual behaviour which is influenced by these chemical messengers. When ants come upon morsels of food they leave a chemical trail to guide other members of the colony to the source. If attacked, a second type of pheromone is secreted which signals the alarm.

Never slow to take commercial advantage of such discoveries, man has incorporated pheromones into many pest control programmes.

In higher animals pheromones are commonly used to identify sexually receptive females – a fact of life only too familiar to dog owners.

At Cambridge University, Dr E. B. Keverne has found that the key factor in triggering sexual activity in rhesus monkeys is pheromones which discriminate between a female's receptive and non-receptive cycles. Even outside the normal fertile period, the overt sexual behaviour of females can be increased by doses of the hormone testosterone, while an absence of appropriate pheromones causes males to ignore their courtship displays. It is also possible for one species of animal to detect fertility related pheromones in others, as shown by American studies in which dogs were trained to detect the special scent produced by a cow on heat.

Pheromones also trigger maternal behaviour by establishing pair bonding in the first few critical moments after birth. In sheep, for example, olfaction draws the ewes to their own young and causes them to ignore any others in the flock. When the mother's sense of smell is deliberately suppressed during pregnancy she can no longer identify her own young. The potency of this bonding has long been put to practical use by shepherds who, by skinning a dead lamb and draping its coat over an orphan, are able to persuade a ewe to accept the youngster as her own.

With such evidence it is hardly surprising that a direct neural connection has been found linking the centre of smell in the brain, the olfactory bulb, with the reproductive system.

Studies of animals have shown that the destruction or removal of this bulb causes the genital glands to atrophy, while the decline of sexual interest in elderly humans is associated with a parallel deterioration in the sense of smell.

Interestingly, Freud attached great significance to the nose as a symbolic sex organ and used this interpretation when analysing his patients' dreams.

Speculation over the precise mechanisms of olfaction – one popular theory held that sensory organs in the nose and mouth distinguished molecules by their infra-red spectrums – was finally ended during the late Sixties by Dr Robert Cagan of the Monell Chemical Senses Center in Philadelphia.

One of the few full-time investigators of the biochemical basis of smell and taste, Robert Cagan showed that the – more than five million – cells lining nasal and oral cavities of animals and fish are equipped with chemical receptors which protrude from their surfaces. As molecules in air and food drift past they are selectively bound to a particular receptor with key in lock precision. 'Sweet' odours, for instance, will only attach to one particular type of receptor. The sensitivity of these cells is so great that just a few molecules of odour are sufficient to trigger a reaction.

Among the most powerful smells is that of ethyl-mercapton – the substance responsible for giving rotten meat its singularly unpleasant odour. Nasal receptors can detect the presence of ethyl-mercapton in amounts of less than one 400 billionth of a gram.

Our senses of smell and taste are the only ones which depend on direct chemical stimulation – vision relies on photons, hearing on vibrations, while touch is triggered by physical contact or temperature changes.

But smell differs in one other extremely significant way from all the other five senses. Whenever our eyes, ears, tongue, or tactile receptors are stimulated, electrochemical impulses are transmitted along nerve bundles, via neuronal gateways, to appropriate areas in the brain. Nerves carrying smell signals are wired directly into the olfactory bulb, and it is from this bulb that the regions responsible for the highest levels of human thought – the cerebral hemispheres – appear to have developed.

In other words the frontal lobes, where such vital functions as memory, the integration of sensory inputs, forward planning, the association between ideas and abstract reasoning occur, evolved directly from smell-processing regions in the primitive brain.

Why the sense of smell alone should convey messages directly into the brain is one of the great mysteries of olfaction research. But the consequences are considerable. Because the signals arrive directly in regions of the brain responsible for memory, for example, we tend to recall memories associated with smells far more accurately, and over much greater periods, than we do those related to sight, sound or touch.

The power of smell to trigger a torrent of recollections is perfectly illustrated by the French novelist Marcel Proust in his *Remembrance of Times Past*. On a cold winter's day, the young Proust accepted a cup of lime tea and a small cake called a *madeleine*. No sooner had he smelled the sweetness of this cake than he was overwhelmed by memories of Combray, the village of his childhood.

Such 'smell' memories have been extensively studied by Professor Trygg Engen of Brown University, who discovered that people were able to distinguish between odours smelled thirty days earlier with 70% accuracy. This compares to a decline of up to 90% for visual or sound memories after a similar period of time.

What made Trygg's findings especially interesting was that he obtained similar results with patients suffering from a form of alcohol-related brain damage known as Korsakoff's syndrome. This is characterised by severe short-term memory deficits, although long-term recollection is only mildly affected and immediate memory remains generally unimpaired. While Korsakoff victims are able to recall childhood incidents clearly and remember anything which has just been said to them, they may be quite incapable of recollecting what they ate for lunch an hour or so earlier. Trygg found that, despite such a major impairment, their memory for scents remains as perfect as before.

The brain's unique ability to detect and remember odours, even when present in only minute quantities, suggests that smell may exert a far more profound influence over human behaviour than has previously been realised.

Furthermore we develop our discrimination for odours at a very early age, as studies by Aidan MacFarlane of the Department of Experimental Psychology at Oxford University have shown. Mothers taking part in the research were asked not to wash or put lanolin ointment on their nipples after feeds and to wear standard gauze breast-pads.

In the second part of the investigation one soiled and one clean pad were placed on a support in such a way that each touched the cheek of a baby, which could turn his or her head by 45 degrees to smell either of the pads. Using this simple device, MacFarlane showed that infants as young as 10 days are not only attracted by their mother's breast odours but can distinguish them from those of strangers.

The discovery of human pheromones occurred in the early Fifties when the French physiologist Jacques Le Magnen was intrigued by the sensitivity of female assistants to exaltolide, a chemical used in perfume manufacture which has a heavy musk-like odour. Whenever they came near a flask of the substance the women became highly aroused and, in some cases, inexplicably upset.

Male colleagues working alongside them were unaffected and, in most cases, unable even to detect the smell. Equally surprising was the fact that sensitivity to the exaltolide varied with the menstrual cycle. Subsequent research showed that sensitivity is at a maximum during ovulation, a fact which enables some women to use it to make an accurate estimation of when they are ovulating. Le Magnen published his findings in 1952, stimulating further research around the world.

The unique nature of human odours is due to the unusual lipid of sebum, an oily secretion of the sebaceous glands composed of fat and skin débris, acted upon by bacteria on the skin's surface. Due to the enormous number of fatty acids our body can produce and because individual variations in enzyme concentrations, the skin's acidity or alkalinity (pH) and temperature all affect the final concentration of each fatty acid, every individual possesses a chemical signature as unique as their finger-prints. This signature is created from a blend of skin, hair, and glandular secretions, of food and drink, and smells absorbed from our surroundings, as well as whatever perfume, after-shave, or deodorant we might have used.

There may also be a genetic factor which causes members of the same family not only to look alike but also to smell alike.

One of the clues which leads many to believe in the potency of odour lies in the curious fact that, although we are not seemingly oversensitive to subtle smells, we are very good at distinguishing between them.

Researchers who asked people to wear T-shirts overnight found they could later not only identify their own but knew which had been worn by men and which by women. In part this seems to have been due to a tendency to attribute stronger and more unpleasant odours to males, and to the fact that, in our culture, most females shave their armpits. This reduces T-shirt odour by preventing a build-up and diffusion of bodily secretions. At the same time the larger male sweat glands produce a greater intensity of body odour.

Exploring the nature of the chemical signature, psychologists gave paper masks to volunteers after misleading them about the nature of their experiment by claiming the masks' purpose was to hide their expressions as they wrote down their attitudes towards candidates in a university election.

Unknown to them the masks had been scented with tiny amounts – so small they were not obviously noticeable – of either androsterone (a hormone found in male perspiration) or vaginal acids, chemicals known to exert a profound effect on the behaviour of lower animals. The question researchers hoped to answer was whether these substances would be capable of influencing attitudes in human subjects.

The results showed that while males were not significantly affected the choice of odours did exert a profound influence on female volunteers. Those exposed to vaginal acids favoured people with a rather shy, retiring approach to the election and disliked dominant or assertive candidates. When the masks contained traces of the male hormone, however, subjects preferred aggressive candidates to those who appeared more passive.

It seems unlikely to be a coincidence, therefore, that males – as noted above – have evolved with large apocrine sweat glands and that their perspiration contains minute amounts of androsterone. Although most human sweat is odourless and serves to regulate body temperature, the specialised apocrine glands, found in the armpits and around the genitals, produce a secretion which contains part of the cells' actual structure. These glands are triggered by emotional responses, including fear, anger and sexual arousal. When acted upon by bacteria the unique body odour is generated. That the apocrine glands are important in sexual behaviour is strongly suggested by the fact that they start functioning around puberty, peak with sexual maturity, and then decline in activity with old age.

Michael Landow found that intact male rats spend much more time investigating the ears and genital organs of both female and castrated rats. He concluded that males use odours, found in the ears and genital region, to distinguish gender. Castration produces odour changes which mislead the intact males into believing they are approaching a female.

To investigate the possible role of pheromones in human physical attraction, researchers have studied the behaviour of species as close to man as possible – monkeys and chimps.

Richard Michael, of the Emery University School of Medicine at Atlanta, Georgia, has spent more than a decade researching the role of pheromones in the sexual activity of monkeys.

He took a group of spayed females, who had previously been ignored by males sharing the same cage, and sprayed their bottoms with vaginal washings from sexually receptive females. Immediately afterwards males fought one another to press the button which raised a barrier between their cage and that housing the treated females. With the obstacle removed the males then repeatedly attempted intercourse, and often succeeded despite the fact that the infertile females did all they could to discourage their unwelcome attentions.

Michael named the pheromone responsible for this behaviour 'copulin' and, by 1971, he had succeeded in isolating the specific chemical which produced the effect. He showed that female rhesus monkeys produce a powerful sex attractant composed of fatty acids which have been modified by the bacteria present in vaginal secretions. More recent work by the same investigators has shown that the same short-chain fatty acids are present in other species of monkeys as well as in humans.

When two women share a room there is a tendency for their menstrual cycles to synchronise. While this might be explained on the basis of other shared factors, for example diet and lifestyle, a study by American psychologist Michael Russell and his colleagues has shown that pheromones serve as a trigger. Using highly absorbent pads, he extracted secretions from the armpits of a female donor. Each morning a small quantity of this substance was placed on the upper lip of other women. In a short space of time their menstrual cycles synchronised with those of the donor they had never met.

Such studies provide support of a mass of anecdotal evidence concerning the powerful effect of odours in sexual attraction. One of the more colourful of these tales recounts the role of scent in the illicit romance between the Marie de Clèves and the Duke of Aragon in 1572.

A royal ball was being held in the Louvre to celebrate the marriage of Marie de Clèves to the Prince de Condet. The 16-year-old bride, described as possessing great beauty and sweetness of nature, 'having danced for a long time and feeling slightly overcome by the heat of the ballroom, went into a dressing-room where one of the Queen's maids helped her to change into a clean chemise'. The Duke, coming by chance into the dressing-room, happened to pick up the discarded chemise and used it to wipe his face. 'From that moment on,' notes Colquet, 'the Prince conceived the most violent passion for her.'

Richard Kraft-Ebbing, the German sexologist, describes how 'A voluptuous young peasant man told me he had seduced quite a considerable number of chaste girls without difficulty by wiping his armpits with his handkerchief while dancing, and then using this handkerchief to wipe the face of his dancing partner.'

In his book *Sexual Behaviour in the Human Female*, the American sex researcher Alfred Kinsey claimed that the frequency and timing of intercourse were primarily a function of male demand and female responsiveness to that demand. More recent research, however, suggests that the key may lie in odours. Naomi Moris and Richard Urdy of the Chicago Medical School tested the effects of a synthetic female pheromone on the sexual behaviour of married couples.

It is known that in humans sexual intercourse peaks during the ovulatory portion of the menstrual cycle. It is also thought that pheromones which act as human copulants peak during the middle of this cycle.

In an earlier study Moris and Urdy found that the probability of intercourse taking place between heterosexual couples was highest at mid-cycle and declined thereafter. What they now wanted to investigate was the role of pheromones in these variations. More than seventy young married couples agreed to take part in the investigation which continued through three of the woman's menstrual cycles. Each woman was given a vial of fluid and asked to apply the contents to her breast at bedtime. Unknown to the couples some of the vials contained a cocktail of aliphetic acids, all of which had been created in a laboratory flask rather than an animal's glands. During the experiment neither the subjects nor the researchers knew whether they were using the potent substance or the placebo. Each morning couples filled out questionnaires in which they described their sexual activities of the previous night. In their first paper, presented to a scientific conference in 1974, Moris and Urdy admitted that – taking the group as a whole – pheromones had no apparent influence on either sexual behaviour or desire. More surprising, however, was the finding that their subjects did not, in general, reveal the anticipated cyclic pattern of infrequency of sexual activity.

Concerned to discover whether these results cast doubt on more than a decade of research, or might be explained by something atypical among that particular group of people, the researchers scrutinised the data provided by the only 12 couples in the sample who followed the expected pattern. Among these subjects they discovered that exposure to pheromones did indeed result in greater sexual interest and activity.

Another American investigator, Richard Doty, has found that the male perception of vaginal odours, in terms of pleasantness and intensity, varies according to the point in the female cycle that samples were taken. In general pre-ovulatory and ovulatory secretions were reported as smelling slightly weaker and less unpleasant than those from the other stages. None of the volunteers considered the odours especially attractive however, although the fact that the experiment was carried out in the laboratory rather than the bedroom may have contributed to that negative perception.

Interestingly, although no evidence was found to link these secretions to human male arousal, they did produce sexual arousal in monkeys. Such cross species reactions are far from uncommon of course, indeed they are the basis of the perfume industry which uses such animal pheromones as musk* in their products.

Perfumes are just one way of emphasising odours, and aerosol sprays containing putative male pheromones are now commercially available – at a price.

One substance used in these products is androstenediol, a chemical structurally related to testosterone, the hormone produced in the testes. Androstenediol, found in the sweat, saliva and urine of the sexually aroused boar, causes a characteristic 'immobilisation reflex' in the sow prior to mating. Its role as a possible human pheromone is suggested by the fact that it is also found in human male urine and sweat.

When researcher Michael Kirk-Smith asked subjects to evaluate photographs, some of which had been sprayed with androstenediol, he found that both males and females rated the sprayed pictures of women as more attractive.

Androstenediol had less influence, however, on judgements about the relative attractiveness of males. Dr David Benton, a leading British researcher in this field, found females reacted more strongly to the hormone during the middle of their monthly cycle when it caused them to assess their own mood as more submissive. He points out, however, that it is very difficult to know whether the effect is pheromonal, or stems from an association between certain odours and particular situations and expectations:

'Sexual attraction relies on many factors including personality, social skills, past experiences and the present situation. If everything else is suitable then an odour may make a small difference but the product of an aerosol spray is unlikely to be the predominant influence and compensate for other failings.'

But what about scents which make no claim to contain human – or animal – derived sex pheromones? Is pure French jasmine essence, the world's most expensive perfume, really worth $200 an ounce?

Part of the answer has been provided by the research of Dr Robert Baron of Purdue University who set out to discover the impact of commercial scent on attraction between male and female college students. To broaden the scope of his enquiry slightly, he decided to devise an experiment which would also consider the association between scent, looks and the way people dress. Dr Baron started by telling his 94 male volunteers that they would be helping investigate the influence of 'first impressions' on character assessment. He then divided his subjects into four groups.

The first met and talked briefly with a female assistant who wore

* Musk, a brown, bitter, volatile substance, comes from a gland near the genitals of the musk-deer and a species of goat found in Tartary. In Persia and Tibet it is eaten as an aphrodisiac.

jeans, a sweater and perfume. The second group spent the same amount of time with a woman wearing skirt, blouse, stockings and the same brand of perfume. Groups three and four met a girl who was either informally, or formally, dressed but did not have any perfume. After their encounters the males completed a questionnaire which explored several characteristics, only some of which were related to personal attraction.

When the answers were examined no difference was found between any of the four groups on those characteristics unrelated to attraction. But the responses to questions about physical appeal revealed some fascinating variations.

Perfume, alone, did not make the woman seem any more attractive. Differences only occurred when both scent and style of dress were taken into account, and then the results were surprising. When the girl wore perfume together with a skirt, blouse and stockings the men considered the female confederate somewhat cold and lacking in romance. Perfume combined with casual clothes, on the other hand, made her appear warmer and more romantic.

Baron then carried out a similar experiment, only this time half the subjects were deliberately provoked by either a male or female confederate, while the remainder had a pleasant encounter. In each group half the confederates wore a pleasant perfume while the others did not.

Following their first meeting the subjects were given an opportunity to respond aggressively to the confederate. When this assistant was male, perfume increased the level of aggression displayed by subjects who had earlier been angered, but it reduced aggression in subjects who had not been provoked. When the confederate was a female, however, the presence of perfume enhanced the amount of aggression expressed whether or not the subjects had experienced provocation.

Overall, the results suggest that people who wear perfume are more likely to become the victims of verbal or physical aggression than those who do not. When a male wearing some kind of perfume is aggressive, the presence of that scent increases the level of aggression used in retaliation. A female wearing perfume risks aggression whether or not she provokes it.

But if smelling sweetly puts you at risk, does an unpleasant odour enhance personal attraction? Research by Robert Baron suggests that, under certain circumstances, a bad smell can make people like one another more. He introduced subjects to one another either in a room with a fresh, pleasant atmosphere or in one which had been polluted by a stink bomb filled with ammonium sulphide. Some of the encounters were between people who closely resembled one another in attitude, a condition which, as we have seen, increases liking at first meeting. Other subjects were not matched for attitude.

Where attitudes were similar, the presence of a smell in the room made the two people express greater liking for one another. Baron believes that it was the sharing of an unpleasant experience which increased attraction.

Are people who spend a fortune perfuming themselves in the hope of adding to their appeal simply wasting time and money?

Despite considerable research over the past two decades the answer must still be that nobody really knows. Certainly the sense of smell is a powerful one in both humans and animals. Nor can there be any doubt about the powerful impact of pheromones on animal behaviour. Researchers caution, however, against generalising their findings in animal studies to anything as complex as human behaviour. It is still doubtful whether pheromones, on their own, do much to enhance personal attraction between humans, who rely more on sight, sound and touch, together with feelings and thoughts, rather than a sense of smell.

My own view is that odours, whether natural or artificial, do have a role to play in triggering and sustaining mutual appeal between two people. But that they exert an influence only within a framework of intricate signals – both verbal and non-verbal – which serve to determine the extent of our loving or loathing.

4

Just good friends

Friend of my infinite dreams
Little enough endures;
Little howe'er it seems,
It is yours, all yours.
Faith hath a fleeting breath,
Hopes may be frail but fond,
But Love shall be Love till death,
And perhaps beyond.

Arthur Christopher Benson
The Gift

Although we may be joined to relatives by ties of blood and to lovers by physical desire, friendships, as the Victorian scholar and poet Arthur Benson* pointed out, are often the most enduring of all relationships.

The final stanza of Tennyson's *In Memoriam*, written in memory of his friend Arthur Henry Hallam who died at the age of 22, perfectly captures their timeless nature:

Far off thou art, but ever nigh;
I have thee still, and I rejoice;
I prosper, circled with thy voice;
I shall not lose thee tho' I die.

* Benson's most enduring work is probably the words for the patriotic song, 'Land of Hope and Glory.'

56

Friendships are found in virtually every human culture and usually highly valued as a social bond.* In American culture especially, intimate relationships between straight males have been glorified in film and folklore, reaching their apogee in the 'buddy' tradition of Huck Finn and Tom Swayer, the Lone Ranger and Tonto, Batman and Robin.

Yet, although friendships may appear to have changed little down the centuries, many experts argue that, as with the modern family, the modern friendship – that 'commerce between equals' as Oliver Goldsmith called it – is of relatively recent origins. According to American psychologists Drs Joseph Bensman and Robert Lilienfeld, its historical roots stretch back only a few centuries to the Renaissance and the Reformation.

It was only then, they argue, with the emergence and growth in importance of individualistic pursuits such as the creative artist and the merchant-trader, that the constricting bonds of family and locality were broken, paving the way for friendships which arose from mutual liking rather than relationships imposed by geography and necessity. Increasingly, friendship became a means of escaping the confines of family life and relationships imposed by occupational roles.

Today it is almost impossible for us to imagine the restrictions, both of physical movement and information, which were the norm during the Middle Ages when communications across large areas of the countryside were almost non-existent and the great majority of people lived a village life of such insularity that any place more than three miles distant was referred to as 'abroad'.

The chief characteristic of medieval society was its absence of individual freedom, with men and women being firmly shackled by their social class. There was as little chance of a person moving from one stratum of society to another as from one village, town or country to the next. Not only did most people die within a few miles of where they had been born, but rigidly enforced conventions dictated how they dressed, what type of food was eaten, where they might sell their wares, and what price could be charged for their labour.

'Personal, economic, and social life was dominated by rules and obligations from which practically no sphere of activity was exempted,' wrote the American psychologist Erich Fromm. Yet

* One exception is the Ik people who inhabit a mountainous region in Uganda. Anthropologist Colin Turnbull reported that their harsh lifestyles and wretched deprivation had created a tribe of fierce and isolated individuals, who knew nothing of co-operation and among whom all forms of love and friendship had been destroyed. Mothers abandoned children to fend for themselves from the age of three, and food was snatched from the dying.

despite this apparent absence of freedom, Fromm also feels there
was little sense of isolation or alienation because each person was
identical with his, or her, social role. You *were* a peasant, knight or
artisan – not an individual who happened to have a particular
occupation.

'Medieval society did not deprive the individual of his freedom,
because the "individual" did not yet exist,' wrote Fromm. 'The
peasant who came into town was a stranger, and even within the
town members of different social groups regarded each other as
strangers.'

The driving force for the social, economic, and philosophical
changes which came about towards the end of the Middle Ages, was
Renaissance Italy. The historian Jacob Burckhardt describes the
Italians of that period as 'the first-born among the sons of Modern
Europe'. The first true individuals.

But such individuality was only purchased at a price. For the
lower classes the dues were collected in a gradual loss of the precise
social roles of feudal times, a dissolution which resulted in the
creation of an anonymous Lumpen proletariat which could more
easily be manipulated and exploited by those in authority. Alongside the concept of individualism, therefore, there also arose the
spectres of tyranny and despotism.

But not even those in positions of power were able to escape from
the consequences of changes which they had helped to engineer.
For their freedom was purchased with the coinage of isolation,
envy, greed, and mutual distrust. The culture of the Renaissance
was that of the rich and the powerful, embodying the pretensions,
ideals and aesthetic values of wealthy nobles and powerful
burghers.

'All human relationships were poisoned by this fierce life-and-
death struggle for the maintenance of power and wealth,' wrote
Fromm. 'Solidarity with one's fellow-men – or at least with the
members of one's own class – was replaced by a cynical detached
attitude . . . the individual was absorbed by a passionate egocen-
tricity, an insatiable greed for power and wealth.' The consequence,
he believes, was an alienation from the self, and an increasing terror
at being alone and vulnerable in a hostile and desperately dangerous
world.

From such fears were forged the early friendships between
autonomous individuals. They offered an escape from the isolation
which individualism had imposed, and provided both opportunities
for mutual aid and mutual protection. Among friends, as with
Alexander Dumas' *Three Musketeers*, it is 'all for one and one for
all'.

In *All Quiet On The Western Front*, Erich Maria Remarque conveys the importance of such mutual aid in times of hardship and danger in his description of the value of a born scrounger to a group of soldier friends: 'We couldn't do without Katczinsky; he has a sixth sense. . . . By trade he is a cobbler, I believe, but that hasn't anything to do with it; he understands all trades. It's a good thing to be friends with him, as Kropp and I are . . .'

This doctrine was developed during the late nineteenth century by such writers as Samuel Smiles and, especially, the Russian author and geographer Peter Kropotkin, who was imprisoned by the French in 1883 for his support of International Working Men's Associations. Throughout the mid-nineteenth and early twentieth century the underlying philosophy of mutual support among friends, expressed in the notion that 'I alone must do it, but I cannot do it alone,' found practical expression in the formation of such organisations as the Friendly Societies, Young Men's Christian Associations (1844), the Fabians (1884) and the growing strength of the trade unions.

While they advanced social, political, religious or ethical causes these provided opportunities for the creation and development of close friendships based on shared values and the common good, while allowing each individual the expression of a personal self, including aspects of that self which might, previously, have been carefully screened from public view. Today this tradition is maintained by a multitude of pressure groups, large and small, which assert the rights of almost every minority from Gay Liberation to One Parent Families.

From its foundation of mutual aid, friendship has grown into an exceptionally complex, intricate and varied phenomenon whose development, maintenance and perhaps eventual ending involves factors not found in any other kind of relationship.

In the largest ever study of friendship – or any other psychological phenomenon for that matter – the magazine *Psychology Today* surveyed its readership to find out exactly how they viewed and experienced relations with others. Some 40,000 readers responded to their questionnaire, providing detailed information about what they looked for, expected from and were prepared to contribute to friendships.

Most highly valued were loyalty, warmth and the ability to keep a confidence, and these were regarded as more important attributes than age, income and occupation.

Not surprisingly, perhaps, people who moved frequently reported having fewer friends than those who had lived for many years in the same neighbourhood.

Less expected, in view of the supposed platonic nature of most friendships, was the finding that nearly a third of those who replied said that they had had sex with a friend in the four weeks prior to completing the questionnaire. This admission makes the finding that 73% regarded opposite-sex friendships as being different from same-sex friendships less surprising.

Friendships between straight and gay men and women were reported by 29% of subjects, and between members of different racial groups by 38%. Little dissatisfaction with the relationships was found, with almost 75% reporting that friendship was reciprocated, that they confided freely in their friends, turned to them in times of emotional upheaval and valued them more as they got older.

Most said they had more close than casual friends and – not unexpectedly – the more friends a person had the less likely he or she was to report feeling lonely.

Friendship was viewed as a form of love by 92%, and 77% were prepared to tell their close friends that they loved them. This high figure is very likely to have been biased by the fact that although the readership of *Psychology Today* is distributed fairly evenly between the sexes, 70% of those responding were female – either because the subject is of greater interest to them, or because women are more willing than men to take the time and trouble to reply to a magazine questionnaire.

Although the results of such surveys should always be treated with a certain amount of caution, a picture emerges of present-day friendship being in good order, with most people well satisfied by its balance of obligations and rewards.

Psychology Today readers appeared to be enjoying a number of predictable benefits from their friendships, advantages of which they were well aware.

But is there more to friendship than that? Could there be hidden benefits of which we remain unaware even while sampling those rewards?

Drs Erik Filsinger and Curtis Anderson of the Arizona State University Centre for Family Studies suspected that an individual's socio-economic class would be of such importance that it would be a major determinant of their own level of self-esteem. If this was so, they reasoned, the effect was more likely to be found among young adults than children. To test their prediction, they gathered together 131 university students whom, they felt, would be in the transition stage between childhood and adulthood.

Self-esteem was measured by determining what the researchers termed 'self-efficacy' or the sense of personal competence. This they assessed using a questionnaire which also asked questions about the parents' social and economic background, as well as that of both their best friend and their best friend's father. Felsinger and Anderson found no correlation between the subject's own status and their sense of self-esteem. But there was a highly significant relationship between the subject's self-esteem and the status of their best friends; findings which were replicated in a later study.

A reasonable interpretation of these results is to demonstrate that people who make friends in a higher socio-economic class are likely to possess strong self-esteem, while those whose friends are drawn from lower socio-economic groups possess less self-esteem.

Despite this, our own social class has little to do with our sense of self-worth, perhaps because we interpret our ability to attract friends of a higher status in terms of our personal competence rather than our background.

It may also be that people already possessing a high self-esteem actively seek out more challenging and complex social interaction – which includes friendships with higher-status others. This finding does, of course, run counter to claims by *Psychology Today* readers that the occupation and income of their friends was of only minor significance. It also emphasises the folk psychology paradox, discussed earlier, which while maintaining that opposites attract also claims that like attracts like. Dr Martin Lea, a social psychologist at the University of Lancaster, has provided a striking example of first argument.

He gave a group of students, who had known one another for some two years, an assessment called the Repertory Grid (REP) Test; we shall be looking at this test and the important psychological concepts behind it later in the book. He also asked them to list their friends on campus. The REP test allows an investigator to measure the nature and extent of feelings which people have for one another and Dr Lea used these results to compare the degree of liking revealed by the Grid with the amount of liking which individuals expressed for one another.

He was especially interested in examining the differences between balanced relationships, where each person expressed an equal amount of friendship for the other, and those unbalanced pairs where one person's liking was not reciprocated.

Dr Lea then listed aspects of attraction under two headings: psychological – which might include warmth, understanding, tolerance, humour; and non-psychological – such as physical appearance, social status and so on.

He found that when friendships were deep and mutual those involved had very similar attitudes, temperaments and personalities. But in an unbalanced relationship the amount of similarity lay somewhere between that found in friendly and unfriendly pairs.

The most interesting finding from this research, however, was the *type* of similarity present. While there might be many shared non-psychological features in a one-sided friendship, significant differences existed at a deeper, psychological level. This means that, in order to have one's friendly overtures returned, it is not sufficient to be superficially similar to the person whose friendship you seek. One must also be like them in personality, attitude and outlook.

Dr Lea believes these results demonstrate that our estimation of both our own and another's personality is of major importance when we make a decision as to whether or not it would be possible or appropriate to make a friend of somebody. Friendships blossom when two people mutually validate feelings about life by expressing very similar views. In the absence of such validation, however, eventual rejection becomes a more likely outcome than a lasting relationship.

Initially the level of similarity sought can be at the relatively superficial level found in lonely heart advertisements of the type: 'Opera-loving, left-wing, non-smoking, vegetarian teacher seeks similar.'

If the advertiser is fortunate somebody sharing his tastes in music, politics, health care and diet will respond. As they spend time together, observing, talking and generally exploring each other's feelings about the world, deeper and more important similarities or differences will appear, enhancing or reducing the chance of a lasting friendship.

Once deep friendships have been formed they tend to be relatively stable unless changes occur in the external conditions which place this friendship network under pressure. One such change may occur when a new friend enters the scene, since every network is a complex system, in which no part can be changed, nor additions made, without it affecting the whole.

Dr Michael Kernis and Ladd Wheeler of the University of Rochester in New York State became curious about the extent to which a newcomer's degree of attractiveness would influence the feelings of other friendship network members towards the individual. Several studies had shown that when a person is paired with a particularly attractive or unattractive member of the opposite sex a 'radiation' effect occurs. That is, people paired with good lookers are perceived more favourably by others on a number of important attributes than those who escort less attractive partners. Kernis and Wheeler decided to see whether the same effect would hold where friends of the same sex were concerned. Lea's work had suggested that a 'contrast effect' might also be possible, where a more attractive friend makes his or her companion appear less attractive and vice-versa.

The experiment was arranged so that subjects would observe a pair of strangers under one of four conditions: in the company of an attractive friend; an unattractive friend; attractive stranger; an unattractive stranger. Their 159 male and female subjects were divided more or less equally into four groups and informed that the study was concerned with exploring the impressions which people make on one another. They were then shown, one at a time, into a waiting-room and introduced to two other people, confederates of the researchers, one of whom – the target – they were asked to assess on a number of attributes of personality and temperament. Since conversations were strictly forbidden, all judgements had to be based solely on visual impressions. The confederates, either both male or both female, were described as either friends or unacquainted, with one of them made up to look either attractive or unattractive. The appearance of the 'target' confederate, about whom the subjects were being asked to form an impression remained unchanged throughout.

The volunteers were asked to rate the target on eleven features, including overall impressions, general liking, degree of confidence shown, physical attractiveness, how friendly the person appeared and so on.

When the pair was presented as strangers, the target was viewed more favourably when accompanied by an unattractive companion than in the company of a good looker, thus confirming the presence of a contrast effect. If the pair was presented as friends, however, the companionship of an unattractive individual caused the target to be viewed *less* positively, so lending support to the radiation effect.

In this situation those making the judgements have to take account of the relationship, and presumably are led to the conclusion that those who can make friends with good-looking people must have favourable qualities which are not immediately apparent. This holds true whether the companion is the same or of the opposite sex.

If you want to be seen as attractive and make the most positive impression on others, therefore, it is essential to ensure your companions are as attractive as possible, a fact which seems to have been appreciated by elderly millionaires and crumbling female film stars long before its triumphant emergence as a scientific conclusion!

Another way in which friendship networks are affected by

changes in our personal relationships was investigated by Drs Michael Johnson of Pennsylvania State University and Leigh Leslie of Fordham University in the United States. They were interested in finding out what happens to friendships when people start dating seriously. Folk wisdom suggests that, as couples become more involved with one another, they withdraw from their social networks and it is tacitly accepted by their former friends that they will be seeing less of them after engagement and marriage.

Johnson and Leslie decided to put this notion to the test among university undergraduates and postgraduate students, a group whom they reasoned would make especially good subjects since separation from families makes social activities an especially important feature of campus life. Information was collected through a questionnaire which used a nine-item 'Love Scale' and included questions about aspects of closeness to and affection for the opposite-sex person most often dated.

In addition the subjects were asked to list their friends and provide information about the importance of each, the extent to which they were prepared to self-disclose to them, the warmth and intimacy of the relationship and so on.

As anticipated, the closer subjects were to their dating partner the more distant, in various ways, they became from their friends, and the fewer friends they possessed, as compared to non-dating individuals. Even more importantly, however, was the change in the *character* of friendships which this brought about. Typically, deeply involved couples attached less importance to their friends' opinions and disclosed less about themselves than did those in casual relationships. The more romantically involved a person became the less significance was attached to former friends, with even the 'best' friend dropping sharply in importance.

Furthermore, the students stated that they talked less with the friend closest to them and with whom, previously, they talked most about personal matters. Even the importance attached to the opinions, attitudes and feelings of near close relatives decreased markedly as the romance bloomed.

Thus friendships, however warm, intimate and important they may have been prior to the development of a mutually close heterosexual involvement will only rarely survive a romance intact and are likely to suffer especially in the months following marriage. This applies not only to casual friendships but also to 'best friends', relationships which those concerned regard as especially important.

But what features distinguish such friendships?

Dr Marjorie Richey of St Louis University set out to find the answer by examining the nature of the bond between close friends among 160 American university students whose ages ranged from 17 to 25. As with other studies a questionnaire was used to obtain detailed information about the start, development and patterns of interaction of same-sex friendships.

Dr Richey found that although only 3% of best friends started out by disliking one another, it took time – between two months and two years – for a 'best friend' relationship to become established. But once the bond is formed, it can be even closer and more intimate than that present in many marriages. She found, for example, that best friends typically confided the most intimate details to one another of their failings, sexual difficulties, financial problems and personal lives. They also passed on information given to them in the strictest confidence by others. Most believed that best friends have the right to advise and criticise one another and confirmed that such advice or criticism was often acted upon.

The best friends in Richey's study demanded a high level of support from one another. For instance more than 50% expected their best friends to stay with them in the event of a bereavement, to lend them up to two weeks' income, and to remain close to them even if they did something unethical. Half the females questioned also believed that their best friend would care for their children if they died.

Best friends were not, however, expected to put their jobs at risk in providing such support.

Only a very few of the friendships, around 6%, came to an end and when this happened it was nearly always because one of the friends was obliged to live some considerable distance from the other. When asked what they thought accounted for the durability of their friendships many cited the ability to be completely themselves as the most important advantage. Other benefits given were a standard against which to measure one's self, a reliable source of support and affection, an understanding and steadfast ally during times of personal crisis.

Although there is nothing especially surprising or even unexpected in Richey's conclusions, one must be careful in generalising these findings across cultures. The powerful 'buddy tradition' already mentioned which prevails in American society may well have biased the results, and intense friendships of this type could prove more typical of the United States than of other countries.

So far we have looked only at friendships between adults, but children have friends as well and many researchers have been interested in trying to find out how they view such relationships. The results suggest that in terms of attitudes, expectations and rewards there is a significant difference between the friendships of children –

especially very young children – and those formed in later life.

According to Drs Robert and Anne Delman of Harvard University, this unique perspective on friendship does not stem from misunderstandings or a lack of information but forms an integral part of their social thinking which tends to be intuitive and seems to flow from a sort of inner knowledge about the way friendships work.

The Delmans base these views on a long and detailed investigation of many hundreds of subjects across an age range from 3 to 45 years, during which special emphasis was placed on the factors which differentiate the friendships of young and old. In their seminal study Robert and Anne Delman discovered that children pass through an orderly sequence of five stages in their understanding of friendships. These appear to be universal and seem similar to the development of other stages of mental growth, in particular to the way in which a sense of morality develops. It must be noted, however, that there is a considerable overlap between the different ages and not every child achieves a perfect transition from one to another. Indeed, as we shall see, some never proceed beyond the third stage and carry infantile ideas about the nature of friendship through to their adult lives.

STAGE 0 Ages 3–7
The Delmans call this stage 'Momentary Playmateship', since it is characterised by attitudes which adults usually perceive as 'selfish'. The child values his or her friends mainly for their material possessions and physical attributes. This focus of interest was perfectly expressed by one of the subjects who, when asked why a particular child was his friend, replied: 'He has a giant Superman doll and a real swing set'.

STAGE 1 Ages 4–9
Here a separation occurs in the child's mind between his own way of looking at the world and the views of others. Friendship is still not regarded as a two-way street, however, which means that notions of give and take or compromise are not a significant feature of such relationships.

Indeed, the Delmans call this the stage of 'One Way Assistance' because the value of a particular friendship is measured in terms of the degree to which one friend does what the other wants.

In other words the needs, views and satisfaction of just one of the pair dominates the relationship and any inability, or reluctance to satisfy such demands can bring the friendship to an abrupt end. One child explained that she had given up being friends with another because: 'She wouldn't go with me when I wanted her to.'

STAGE 2 Ages 6–12
Termed the 'Two-Way Fair Weather Cooperation Stage' by the
Delmans, it represents a large step towards the establishment of
what adults would view as a friendship. Here the child starts to see
friendship as being a two-way street so that give-and-take becomes a
more important feature of the relationship. In this stage children are
concerned about what their friends think of them and a friendship is
not seen as progressing satisfactorily unless both are participating
and benefiting to a similar extent. However the selfish notions of
friendship have not entirely disappeared and friends may still
be primarily valued according to their ability to satisfy a child's
personal needs.

STAGE 3 Ages 9–15
This stage is characterised by the acquisition of objectivity and
empathy on the child's part. He, or she, starts to understand the
feelings of others and is able to step outside friendships and take a
third-person view of their functioning. It has been called the stage of
'Mutually Shared Relationships', since there is a growing emphasis
on reciprocal helping with a working towards interests which, while
both share, are independent of each of them. Friends begin to share
feelings and help one another through personal conflicts and difficulties. The stress is on intimacy rather than the mutual satisfaction of needs.

STAGE 4 Ages 12 and older
Called the stage of 'Autonomous Independent Friendships', this
final phase of development is marked by the acceptance of an equal
need for autonomy and dependency in their friendship which
permits friends to develop independent relationships without the
bond being damaged.

The Delmans consider that these stages are organised in such a
way that the child acquires greater and greater insight while passing
through them. Although a child may clearly be in one of the higher
stages, this does not mean that he, or she, has completely shaken off
all the attitudes characteristic of the earlier stages and may revert
back to these from time to time. As we have already explained the
ages given only provide an approximate indication of the point at
which a child moves from one stage to the next, since development
is never that predictable.

The Delmans found, for example, that many adolescents had
great difficulty in moving from stage 3 to stage 4 despite the fact that
they had entirely rejected the intimate closeness of the earlier stage.
This seemed to produce a crisis in that they were torn between the

desire for independent relationships and the need for those in which they could be certain of a comfortable interdependency. Indeed there are many adults who never seemed to have progressed beyond the third stage or, like Delmans teenagers, to have been firmly stuck between that and stage 4.

It seems likely that adult friendships develop in a similar way with first impressions corresponding to the 0 stage with physical appearance or material benefits being of primary importance. As familiarity increases, stages 1 and 2 are passed through with each discovering the other's likes and dislikes while both derive increasing satisfaction from one another's company. There follows a period of increasing self-disclosure and other expressions of intimacy before the relationship occasionally matures into the state of autonomy implied by stage 4. Even before stage 4 is reached, however, a couple may find themselves becoming more than just good friends.

5

Sex, love and marriage

'There can be no peace of mind in love, since the advantage one has secured is never anything but a fresh starting point for further desires.'

Marcel Proust *Remembrance of Times Past*

Humans are the sexiest animals on earth. The only species free to engage in sex at all times, without the restraints imposed by reproductive necessity. Little wonder then that friendships should all too often be the starting point for a relationship of greater intimacy. To exchange, what Oliver Goldsmith defined in *The Good Natured Man* as a 'disinterested commerce between equals' for what he derided as 'an abject intercourse between tyrants and slaves'.

An American psychologist, Dr Jeffrey Young of the University of Pennsylvania, have even devised a 'Love Formula', a mathematical equation which helps you to work out how many months it is going to take you to track down the perfect partner. According to his calculations the sum of human sexuality looks like this:

$$\text{Number of months to wait} = \frac{0.7}{O \times S \times A \times D \times I}$$

Here, O stands for Opportunity, the number of eligible partners you meet per month. S represents Selectivity, the proportion you find attractive. A equals the proportion of those you decide to Approach. Desirability, D, is the proportion of those you fancy who fancy you in return and agree to date. I, the Intimacy factor, refers to the proportion of first dates that develop into a relationship lasting at least six months. Finally 0.7 stands for the 70% probability that the equation will turn out to be true.

Suppose, for instance, you meet 8 new people per month and find half of them attractive. You approach a quarter of these and get your request for a date accepted 50% of the time. Your track record shows that one out of ten dates leads to a more lasting relationship.

Now the formula tells you that the number of months you must wait before meeting Mr or Ms Right is:

$$\frac{0.7}{8 \times 0.5 \times 0.25 \times 0.5 \times 0.1} = \text{approximately 14 months.}$$

Suppose, however, you manage to meet two more potential partners a month. The number of months you need to wait now reduced to 11. Become a bit more sociable, double the number of eligible dates you meet and your waiting time is slashed to a mere 7 months.

Jeffrey Young developed his mathematical solution to mating after researching the reasons why some people take several years to find romance, while others manage it in far less time. He found that attractiveness was less important than the 5 factors included in his formula, the opportunity to meet eligible partners, how selective people were when seeking out a partner, how many of those they found attractive were actually approached, their own desirability and their skill at turning an initial meeting into the first of many dates.

Although fairly lighthearted, this formula does serve a serious purpose in therapy. Young explains that merely telling a lonely, loveless client that he, or she, was too selective didn't have the same impact as mathematically demonstrating the mathematical improvement in their chances if they met a few more new people each month, or raised their approach rate by a few percent.

FALLING IN LOVE

While maths may provide us with the probability of somebody making out on a Saturday night, it has, fortunately, nothing to say on the subject of falling in love. That moment when reason is abandoned, blind passion rules and, as James Joyce wrote: '. . . then I asked him with my eyes to ask again yes, and then he asked me would I yes . . . and first I put my arms around him yes and drew him down to me so he could feel my breasts all perfume yes and his heart was going like mad and yes I said yes I will yes.'

Yet, as Robert Solomon says in *The Passions*, much of what passes for love is not love at all, but a yearning for security or a desire for dependency '. . . the often resentful ties that bind us without elevating us and set us against each other rather than draw us together. Love is the ideal of all of us; intimacy and mutually elevating equality, complete trust and maximum esteem for both ourselves and others.'

But so far as some psychiatrists and biochemists are concerned passion may produce the same effect on the brain as a powerfully addictive narcotic. 'At a neurochemical level attachment is essentially an addictive phenomenon involving opiods,' says Jaak Panksepp, professor of psychology at Ohio's Bowling Green State University.

Experiments with opiods, the brain's equivalent of opiates, have shown that when young animals, puppies, guinea pigs and chicks are taken from their normal surroundings, separation anxiety can be prevented by administering two types of narcotic, beta endorphins and clonidine, a drug used for reducing the severity of withdrawal symptoms when treating drug addicts. These opiates act not by sedating the animal but, researchers believe, by inhibiting the neural circuits concerned with anxiety arousal. This has led to the suggestion that attachment, not only in all animals, including humans, may be based on an addiction to these drugs. Attachment by stimulating the production of these opiates, leads to a form of natural addiction. Once the attachment is lost, however, the brain is starved of its regular 'fix' and produces responses similar to those found in drug deprived addicts.

Biologically, this addiction would have the evolutionary advantage of keeping pairs of animals bonded for long enough to raise their young. It could explain the depth of the emotional anguish and even physical pain resulting from the ending of a close relationship, as well as accounting for the changes in behaviour, often extreme and sometimes bizarre, that result from falling 'head over heels' in love. This 'giddy high' is likened by New York psychiatrist Dr Michael Liebowitz to a shot of amphetamine. In some cases people may become so hooked on these feelings that they become virtual 'love junkies' racing from encounter to encounter and from one relationship to the next in a desperate attempt to satisfy their addiction to the romantic fix. As a result, they seldom care very much who they are falling in love with, and usually have a background of disastrous relationships.

Dr Donald Klein, of the New York State Psychiatric Institute, speculated that this kind of frantic romancing might be linked to the brain's production of phenylethylamine, a brain chemical that acts in the same way as amphetamine. Michael Liebowitz tested his colleague's theory by administering a male 'love junkie' with an anti-depressant drug called a Mono-Amine Oxidase inhibitor (MAO). This suppresses the breakdown of phenylethylamine, and so prevents it from affecting brain function. Within a few weeks his love addicted patient had settled down to a more normal pattern of attraction. 'He no longer got so carried away by romance,' the doctor remarked. 'The frantic need to have somebody all the time vanished.'

Even in men and women whose patterns of behaviour are less extreme, that first moment of attraction triggers a powerful biochemical response. As the novelty wears off, however, couples usually pass into the second attachment phase of their relationship. During this time rather different, less intense but no less pleasurable emotions are experienced, feelings which help to cement the bond between them. Once again the chemistry of love exerts a potent influence over feelings and behaviour. 'At this stage,' says Dr Liebowitz, 'the presence of a loved one no longer heightens arousal but has a calming influence, inducing a sense of general well-being.'

He regards these two stages of loving, *attraction* and *attachment*, as biologically determined and involving two distinct neural mechanisms. Just as men and women can get hooked on the first stage of love, so too can they become addicted to the attraction phase, clinging tenaciously to a relationship, even though it brings them only unhappiness and extreme distress should it come to an end. Indeed studies have shown that the end of even the most miserable relationship can lead to symptoms very similar to those seen in a junkie being forced to cold turkey the habit.

Such people, Dr Liebowitz believes, may produce too few opiods and so cling with barnacle-like persistence to their mates to prevent these neurochemicals from falling below the critical level at which panics occur.

This discussion of neurochemicals and love junkies may seem far removed from the pure passions of the Song of Solomon or the tender romance of Romeo and Juliet. Yet it seems positively mystical compared with the hard-nosed theories of the 'naked ape' school of socio-biology. Biochemists at least are prepared to recognise the human as an animal. Some socio-biologists grant our species the status of mere biological mechanisms, gene machines programmed from foreplay to orgasm for the sole purpose of reproduction. According to this view, falling in love, or 'pair bonding' to use the preferred expression has nothing to do with poetry, little to do pleasure and everything to do with procreation.

A version of their theory runs like this. When humankind first rose on its hind quarters and began to walk on two legs rather than four, evolution led to radical changes in structure. In the male the penis detached from the stomach allowing him, as one anthropologist expressed it to me, to 'piss without having to stand on his head.' The eyes moved to the front of the face to provide the binocular vision needed if distances are to be accurately estimated – an essential skill when you spend much of your time swinging from tree to tree.

Bipedal mobility placed great strains on the pelvis which had to be strengthened to prevent it cracking under the slightest shock. For males this presented no problem, but as the female pelvis grew stronger the birth canal also became smaller, by a factor of one or two diameters. A smaller birth canal meant that a baby with a large head would remain forever trapped in the womb.

Some protohominids overcame this problem by producing more immature infants with heads small enough to squeeze through the narrower canal. Immature infants, being more helpless than mature ones, have to be looked after for much longer if they are to survive. This required the development of pair bonding mechanisms which would keep the couple together for the necessary amount of time.

When this idea from anthropology is linked to one from genetics, a concept emerges which may explain – at least in biological terms – much everyday social behaviour.

In *The Selfish Gene*, Richard Dawkins describes the accidental formation, in the primeval soup of four thousand million years ago, of a 'remarkable molecule' which he calls the *replicator*. As the name suggests, this molecule had the ability to make copies of itself. 'Replicators began not merely to exist, but to construct for themselves containers, vehicles for their continued existence,' he explains. 'The replicators which survived were the ones which built *survival machines* for themselves to live in.'

Today we call these replicators genes. They are, says Dawkins, the building blocks from which mind and body are created. 'We are their survival machines.'

So the argument goes like this. Pair bonding was necessary because of the long maturation period required by the human neonate, born more immature than any other mammal due to the necessity to pass through a narrowed birth canal. But this neonate was more than just the apple of its parent's eyes. He, or she, was also a newly minted survival machine, packed with genes whose sole evolutionary purpose was the propagation of their particular genetic brand.

Following this line of thinking to its logical conclusion provides an explanation for the promiscuous, adulterous, male. However despicable his behaviour in social terms, biologically he is just doing what comes naturally. By impregnating as many females as possible with his sperm, his genes stand the best possible chances of survival. If he can then persuade another male to invest time, energy and effort raising this cuckoo in the nest as his own, the advantages are even greater. Not only will his genes be advantaged, the rival males will be disadvantaged.

Where mating is concerned, this theory suggests that humans may well be influenced in their attractions by the genes' survival programme. In a woman, the male will look for features which suggest she can successfully bear many children. The woman, however, will be searching out clues that suggest he is going to be constant and true, that her chosen partner will stick by her during the years of child raising. As a result, it is argued, men are more interested in physical cues while women are more concerned with character and personality.

MARRIAGE VOWS

As thousands of couples discover each year, falling out of love is often a great deal easier than falling in love. And while one marriage in three ends with divorce, many more deteriorate into the mutual misery of lives shared for the sake of the children or because couples simply can't afford the cost of living apart.

But why should one relationship flourish while another fails? What does it take for two people not merely to stay together but grow closer as the years go by? While there is no such thing as the recipe for the ideal marriage, partnerships which work well do seem to have certain features in common.

An ability to mirror some of their partner's attitudes and complement others appears to be an important element in most long lasting relationships. But while this provides a firm foundation on which to build a relationship, it does not mean that their feelings will survive unscathed as they pass through the three critical stages of married life during which togetherness is severely tested.

Surprisingly, perhaps, crisis point number one occurs during the very first year of marriage, a time when the world thinks of most couples as being blissfully happy and very much in love. Ironically it is a belief in this myth which often makes matters worse as it blinds the newly weds to difficulties within their relationship.

74

Still captivated by the 'happy couple' image of their wedding day, they may be unwilling to recognise that problems can arise and reluctant to discuss their feelings openly with one another. Instead they tend to fall back on misguided optimism: 'I'm sure it will work out alright . . .' and comforting self-deceptions: 'If I'm only patient he's bound to see things my way!'

Surviving this first crisis largely depends on the couple's ability to recognise and deal with problems as they arise and to discuss even the most intimate details of their relationship frankly and freely. To do this each must trust the other and feel certain that honest admissions are never going to be stored away for use as ammunition in some future fight.

Crisis time number two arrives not after seven years of marriage, as the myth of the seven year itch would have us believe, but a couple of years later. The chief dangers here arise from boredom and complacency as couples start taking one another for granted and smugly assume that nothing could ever harm such an established relationship.

You can test the emotional warmth of your own marriage – no matter how long it has lasted – by answering these questions:

* Do you criticise your partner in front of guests or the children?
* Do you believe separate holidays are a good idea?
* Do you call each other Mummy and Daddy instead of your names?
* Do you believe that affection is best left to intimate moments?
* Do you feel uncomfortable giving each other a kiss and a cuddle for no good reason other than to show affection?

If your answer to all of them was a decisive 'no' you are still emotionally close to your partner and showing it. Less than three 'no' responses however, and you could be drifting apart.

Discontent during this period is often accompanied by feelings of guilt and a sense of betrayal over not finding your partner as exciting and attractive as you once did. This may result in a frantic search for that elusive something which will put the magic back in your relationship.

In this quest for the perfect partnership, unfavourable comparisons may be made between one's own marriage and those of friends and neighbours. 'Maybe I'm too dependent,' worries one woman, believing that only by being assertive can she revitalise her marriage. 'Perhaps I'm too independent,' reflects a male, believing that he can rediscover the tenderness of earlier years only by growing more clinging.

It may be that some sort of dramatic change is indeed needed to refresh a stale relationship. But the mistake here is to assume that because something works well for one couple, it's bound to be just as effective in your own relationship.

Staying together depends on accepting that, since you are both unique individuals, nobody else ever will, or ever can, experience exactly your emotions or possess precisely the same needs. Which means that solutions have to be found within your own relationship rather than inside somebody else's. This doesn't mean never seeking advice or talking things over with others. Very often an outsider's view helps put things into perspective and talking to a sympathetic friend can help you think about your ideas more clearly. But unhappy marriage partners should never lose sight of the fact that there are no perfect answers and copying somebody else's approach to married life is most unlikely to prove successful in the long run.

Around this time many couples assume that each must know of the other's feelings without having to be shown or told. Nothing could be further from the truth. While women may well value spontaneous gestures of affection more than many men, even the most macho male needs the reassurance of a warm hug or unexpected kiss from time to time.

The third and final critical period occurs as a couple reach their mid to late forties and attempt to prove to themselves – or to each other – how youthful and attractive they have remained. Either partner, although it is more often the man, may seek out a young, attractive, companion to flatter his vanity and boost his ego. Essential for the survival of a relationship during this crisis are tolerance, understanding and the wisdom to know when to speak out and when to stay silent. Bitter debates and endless recriminations only widen the gulf while silence sometimes manages to bridge it.

In later life, as a close relationship matures into a deep and loving friendship, many couples echo the words of Robert Browning: 'Grow old along with me, the best is yet to be . . .' as they discover them to be the most richly rewarding years of all.

GAY LOVE

Many of the factors involved in physical attraction, be they biological or psychological, apply to homosexual as much as to heterosexual relationships. Gay men and women are not alien beings unique in their emotional responses and feelings, separated by their sexual orientation from the rest of humanity, but perfectly ordinary men and women whose choice of partners is just one facet of their being. Homosexuality is not even biologically unusual, many other species adopt the same mode of behaviour under various conditions.

None the less, the question of why people should be attracted to their own sex is an intriguing one. It is also, unfortunately, a riddle without an adequate answer.

Currently there are two opposing and extreme solutions on offer, neither of which does justice either to science or human diversity.

The first has echoes of John Locke's view that at birth the mind of each individual is a blank slate, a *tabula rasa* on which experience writes the script. According to this view sexual preferences are not preordained, although sexual desires, just like hunger and thirst, are innate physiological mechanisms. Just as culture determines what, when and where we shall eat and drink, so do social mores profoundly influence sexual orientation. According to the American sociologist John Gagnon, for example, boys grow to like girls because that is what their family, friends, neighbours, relatives and society at large expect them to do.

This approach suggests that sexual orientation is acquired, like any other learned response, through a process of rewards and punishments or, to use the language of behaviourism, reinforcement. A child does something and learns whether or not to repeat that action, and the frequency with which it should be repeated, through the consequences. A desirable reinforcement, approval, physical and emotional pleasure encourages the same response at a later date. Punishment, not surprisingly, makes it less likely the same activity will be repeated.

The opposite view, which psychiatrist Dr D. J. West has termed the 'Sleeping Beauty' theory, claims that sexual responses appear fully developed when the appropriate stimulus appears. 'We know of course,' he comments 'that this happens only in fairy tales.' Indeed, research by Michael Schofield has shown that most adolescents find their first experience of sexual intercourse unsatisfactory and disappointing.

Human behaviour is, needless to say, a great deal more subtle and complex that either of these extreme views and the truth probably lies in a complex mixture between them. That is in an interaction between nature and nurture.

Let's consider some of the evidence on both sides of the debate. If the blank slate theory is true, one might expect early homosexual experiences between boys, or girls, to exert a profound effect on their later life. Indeed one of the motivating fears of legislators and others who seek to keep homosexual male teachers out of schools is that they will corrupt and, thereby, permanently impair the sexual orientation of boys under their care. This view, which owes more to prejudice than rationality, overlooks a number of vital points.

Firstly there is no evidence that homosexual male teachers are any more likely to seduce boys than that heterosexual male teachers will sexually molest their girl students.

Secondly, even when such assaults do occur there is very little evidence in support of the view that homosexual experiences in adolescence permanently change a male's orientation. Kinsey's first serious study of the male homosexual, published in 1948, suggested that while 37% of American men had at least one homosexual experience leading to orgasm by the age of 45, only 4% of them were exclusively homosexual. Prisons, single-sex public schools, military establishments, or any other institutions which deny access to women, will result in previously heterosexual males seeking sexual relief with other men. Yet removed from these situations their original preference is immediately re-established.

In other cultures no stigma attaches to relationships between men and boys, nor does the attachment lead to fears that it will produce a permanent change in orientation. In ancient Greece, especially in the Doric states, it was a custom that every man attracted to him a boy or youth for whom he became not only a lover but also friend, guardian and counsellor. According to historian Hans Licht: 'It was recognised so much as a matter of course by the State that it was considered a violation of duty by the man, if he did not draw one younger to him, and a disgrace to the boy if he was not honoured by the friendship of a man.'

The debate between inborn and acquired homosexuality goes back to the mid-nineteenth century when a certain Dr Casper proposed that the majority of homosexuals were suffering from a congenital abnormality rather than any 'depraved fancy'. Others, however, had acquired a taste for the 'vice' as a result of 'oversatiety with natural pleasures.' Such men, Dr Casper cautioned, 'indulge their gross appetites alternately with either sex.'

To recognise the long-term, born pederast one had only to examine the rectum since frequent sodomy brought about clearly identifiable changes to its appearance. Casper, and other medical men, produced several learned papers on this subject, debating the vexed question of whether a funnel-shaped rectum and lack of radial folds were the invariable results of anal intercourse and might be regarded as legal proof of it.

Yet Casper, for all his speculations on the gay rectum, was in many ways an innovative doctor with ideas ahead of his time. As Arno Karlen points out in *Sexuality and Homosexuality*: 'He was one of the first scientists to stress that some homosexuals felt true love for each other' – even, he said 'a warmth of passion more fervent than is common in the relation of the opposed sexes'. He also broke convention by pointing out that homosexuality and sodomy are not synonymous, for many homosexuals never in their lives experience anal intercourse.'

In 1862 a German homosexual lawyer, Karl Heinrich Ulrichs, began writing the first of many books and pamphlets in which he tried both to explain and to defend homosexuality. At first he published these under the pseudonym Numa Numantius, but later was courageous enough to use his own name.

The human embryo, said Ulrichs, begins life without any sexual differentiation, and only assumes a gender a few months after conception. In homosexuals, he claimed, the embryo physically differentiated into a male, and developed male genitalia, but in that part of the brain responsible for determining sexual orientation, differentiation did not occur. The result was a female soul trapped in a male body. Fifty years later Freud adopted a similar argument to explain his belief that everyone has a latent homosexual drive.

Since the term homosexual had not been coined at the time Ulrichs was writing, and he rejected pederast or sodomite, it was necessary for him to coin a new word. In Plato's *Symposium* he read that males dedicated to the goddess Urania are especially attracted by other men. Ulrichs Germanised Urania to *urning*, creating a noun which was to be widely used for half a century.

Ulrichs considered homosexual love as pure and elevating as heterosexual love and strenuously rejected the view that homosexual men were either sick or suffering from a congenital abnormality.

Some 7 years after Ulrich published his first book, a Hungarian named Benkert, writing under the name Kertbeny, coined the term homosexual, from the Greek *homos* meaning 'same'.

At the time his paper attracted little interest or attention, but the same year, 1869, saw the publication in the Berlin academic journal *Archiv fur Psychiatrie* of a report by the eminent neurologist Karl Westphal on transvestism, describing what he termed 'contrary sexual feelings' as a form of moral insanity resulting from the 'congenital reversal of sexual feelings.'

Other doctors and psychiatrists responded with interest to his ideas and began to submit further papers. In less than ten years a trickle of interest turned into a tidal wave of academic enthusiasm, with some of the most respected psychiatrists of their day joining in the debate. But the sum total of these luminaries' contributions added little to the stature of science and absolutely nothing to that of the homosexual.

According to Dr Moreau homosexuals were the link 'between

reason and madness' whose affliction could be explained 'by one word: Heredity'. In their paper *Inversion of the Genital Sense* the eminent Drs Charcot and Magnan identified the cause of the problem as a constitutional weakness of the nervous system resulting from congenital degeneration. Their paper added to the literature the words 'invert' and 'inversion.' August Forel, a Swiss researcher, agreed with the opinion that homosexuals were not monsters of vice but victims of their genes and added the additional information that 'The excesses of female inverts exceed those of the male. One orgasm succeeds another, night and day, almost without interruption.'

So far as the beleaguered homosexual was concerned, the only up side to this universally stigmatising diatribe was that most open-minded medical men advocated consignment to mental hospitals for treatment rather than to prison for punishment.

In 1893 Lombroso contributed his measure of ignorance to the discussion by claiming, in his book *The Female Offender*, that many prostitutes and female criminals were usually 'mannish', so implying a link between criminality, prostitution and lesbianism. Today the trend seems to have swung back to seeing homosexuality more as a learned response, perhaps acting on an innate predisposition. This implies that the sexual roles each of us comes to enact in life are cast not by nature but by nurture. One of the most vigorous exponents of this view is the American psychologist John Money, a leading expert on sex-roles and author of a major work on sexual stereotyping *Man, Woman, Boy and Girl*. Far from regarding psychological differences as immutably programmed by genes, he claims there are only four imperative differences between the sexes: 'Women menstruate, gestate and lactate,' he says, 'men impregnate.'

In October 1963, a young American couple drove with their identical twin boys to a local hospital for what should have been the routine and relatively minor operation of circumcision by means of an electric cauterising needle. Routine turned to tragedy, however, when as the doctor was operating on the first child, a surge of current burned off the infant's penis. Desperate for a way of coping with this catastrophe, the parents sought advice from psychologists whose suggestion was to raise the boy as a girl. Today, aided by plastic surgery and reared as their daughter, the child has developed into a well adjusted young adult who is, psychologically at least, a female.

Another case cited in medical literature described how an infant with a rudimentary penis and other genital defects was 'assigned' as a boy by physicians because he had two testes and the chromosome make-up of a male.* When the child was 17 months old it was decided that his best chance of happiness lay in reassigning him as a girl. Surgery and hormones formed part of the treatment, but of far greater importance was the change in attitudes towards the infant by members of the family. An older brother was asked to help the child establish a feminine identity and soon the parents were reporting a newly protective attitude towards the infant he now regarded as his sister. 'Before he was just as likely to stick his foot out and trip her as she went by,' commented the father. 'Now he wants to hold her hand to make sure she doesn't fall.'

In their regular consultations with specialists at the John Hopkins Psychohormonal Research Unit, who supervised the upbringing of the boy who lost his penis, the parents mentioned fairly rapid changes in behaviour between the twins. Only a few months after starting to treat the boy as a girl the mother told the clinic: 'She doesn't like to be dirty. Maybe it's because I encourage it, she is very proud of herself when she puts on a new dress and she just loves to have her hair set. Our son is quite different, I can't wash his face for anything.'

In both these cases the effects of conditioning, not only on the children but on the family as a whole, are graphically illustrated. The older brother, who clearly received a certain measure of encouragement when aggressing against another male, quickly realised that such conduct would not be acceptable if directed against his 'sister'. As a result he began to respond in a more 'protective' (i.e. stereotypically masculine) manner towards her. Similarly, the parents of the second child adopted different criteria for what was acceptable behaviour by each of their two children. In both cases it seems likely that the pressures employed to bring about these changes were more often subtle than obvious, involving a larger number of non-verbal than verbal indications of approval, encouragement, support and acceptance. For it is by silent speech as much as the spoken word that patterns of learning are established through the proffering or withholding of a reward.

Two case histories, which well illustrate this powerful desire to conform to social norms, concern the families of hermaphrodites. Each child possessed a female chromosome pattern at birth, i.e. 2 XX chromosomes. Each had internal female organs, together with a penis and empty scrotum externally.

One family considered their child a girl and raised her accord-

---

* Both sexes inherit 44 chromosomes determining non-sexual characteristics plus 2 sex chromosomes, XY for males; XX for females.

ingly, using surgery and hormones to make her appearance conform to the chosen sex. The other parents raised their child as a boy. By the time she reached adolescence the girl had a steady boy friend and expected to marry, while the boy had a girl friend and found no problem adjusting to the male role in marriage.

As they grew up, these children like the majority of others, looked to social and family models for answers about what to think and how to behave. It is there that the homosexual child, whether or not he or she is fully aware of their sexual orientation, faces a problem. One which may produce severe psychic conflict, create self-doubt and generate a crisis of identity. For the gay young person there are usually no appropriate role models to guide behaviour. On the contrary, those models which society and the family do provide are often at odds with that individual's emotional responses to life. As a result they are obliged to develop not only in the absence of a powerful learning influence but within an environment that is frequently uncomprehending, unsupportive and grossly insensitive to their needs. Not only are they denied the guidance and social validation for their attitudes and behaviour which the heterosexual child secures from adults and peers, but made more uncertain and anxious by an inability to conform – if only emotionally – to those widely accepted norms.

This is not to assert that the heterosexual's models are essentially valid since, in many instances, they are dangerously deceptive fabrications created largely in order to exploit teenage aspirations. The highly coloured and grossly unrealistic images of romance and marriage propagated by magazine publishers and television advertisers, for instance, provide idealistic roles that adolescents will strive for in vain. One reason, perhaps for the high rate of marriage break-down already mentioned.

For the gay girl or boy attempts to conform to socially acceptable roles in life and to satisfy parental expectations will lead to increasing conflict as the realisation of their sexual orientation becomes more clearly established. The question: 'How does a boy (or girl) behave in this situation?' then produces an answer that clashes with powerful feelings about their inner selves. The divergence between Real Self and Ideal Self, mentioned in chapter one, leads to a psychological state of tension, anxiety, and self-doubt which psychologist Leon Festinger has termed *cognitive dissonance*, also discussed in chapter two.

Dissonance arises for the homosexual youth when behaviour which to them seems not only normal and natural but vitally necessary to their development as human beings, is condemned by society as unnatural, unacceptable and entirely unnecessary. Such dissonance can be resolved in only one of two ways: by changing orientation or altering attitudes towards it.

The former is a route travelled by many homosexuals who refuse to acknowledge that their primary preference is for members of their own sex. This need for conformity may lead to marriage and even raising a family, even though the relationship never strikes them as quite 'right' or entirely satisfying.

Dissonance can also be reduced, without the need to suppress homosexual behaviour, by devising explanations for their orientation which appear more 'socially acceptable' to themselves if not to others. A young male, living with a partner who is older and more prosperous may tell himself: 'I'm only here for the security. One day I'll leave him and find a girlfriend.' A gay teenager in a single-sex school may attribute his interest to an absence of females and feel he will 'grow out of it'. The male who wakes up after a 'one night stand' with another man may claim to have been too drunk at the time to know what he was doing.

That such reasons are advanced to reduce dissonance does not, of course, mean they are invalid and always founded in self-deception. Sexuality is a continuum rather than two separate and mutually incompatible responses. To enjoy healthy psychological adjustment, however, it is important to gain sufficient self-awareness and objectivity to recognise the validity or otherwise of such rationales and not employ them as a smokescreen for concealing unpalatable truths.

Another way of reducing dissonance is by membership of a group which offers a distinctive and relatively easily copied role model. By doing so they are able to reject the majority view, discovering the support and validation denied them by the world at large in the company of like minded others.

Paradoxically this search for emotional security may lead to them adopting the stereotyped roles which heterosexual society holds true of all homosexuals, camp males, butch females and leather boys. But this is irrelevant to them since they have already rejected society's views and the more stereotypic the role to be followed the easier, in many ways, it is to adopt. This is simply because the message is put across so vividly and clearly that it is hard to make a mistake when attempting to achieve conformity.

Once one has adopted a particular role, grown familiar with the demands it makes, experienced the rewards it offers and learned to tolerate any penalties it produces and internalised the social skill that determines how the part shall be played, it no longer becomes a role at all. It is the real You, the genuine, 100% sincere individual identity. Because it now seems so 'natural', other life styles that might cheerfully have been adopted given a different set of circumstances can appear strange, incomprehensible or distasteful. The homosexual who prefers to live in conformity with the expectations of the heterosexual world, so far as this is possible, may repudiate the very camp or very butch gay. The advocate of Gay Liberation is likely to brand the conformist homosexual a 'closet queen' and charge the bisexual with self-deception. The macho leather male may express contempt for the transvestite, the transvestite mock the muscle man.

To some extent such a rejection of other people's lifestyles is probably inevitable, since one way of supporting your own position is to devalue the position of others. The more powerful the attack the greater the self-doubt and underlying sexual uncertainty on the part of those who originate it.

In *Remembrance of Times Past*, Marcel Proust gave clear expression to the feelings of both heterosexual and homosexual men and women struggling to make sense of the conflicting emotions aroused by love.

'What we suppose to be our love or our jealousy is never a single, continuous and indivisible passion. It is composed of an infinity of successive loves, of different jealousies, each of which is ephemeral although by their uninterrupted multiplicity they give us the impression of continuity, the illusion of unity.'

In this chapter I have looked at some usually overlooked aspects of sex and love. In the next we shall explore the second of Proust's two passions – jealousy. That corrosive emotion which, often in the guise of love or the name of friendships, can end by destroying both.

6

Sins of the fathers

Portraits of youths, masculine names, annoy me;
I hate the cradle holding a baby boy;
I hate her mother when she gives her kisses,
her sister, and the girl who sleeps with her;
I hate them all – forgive me – I am timid
and I suspect a man in every smock.

Sextus Aurelius Propertius (c. 51BC)

Of all the emotions aroused by personal attraction, jealousy –
Shakespeare's 'green-ey'd monster which doth mock the meat it
feeds on' – is the most painful and potentially destructive. In
Paradise Lost, Milton describes it as creating the 'injured lover's
hell', and to Dryden it was the 'tyrant, tyrant Jealousy'. In the *Old
Testament* its cruelty was likened to that of the grave, while for
Bertrand Russell it was 'the great vice which poisons human
relations'.

Certainly those savage consequences of jealousy: suspicion, distrust, bitterness, blind fury have profoundly affected not only the
lives of individuals, but the course of history itself. Yet, as we shall
see, jealousy cannot be considered a useless or entirely negative
force since, in evolutionary terms, the emotion has much to com-
mend it.

One of jealousy's most striking features is its universality, being found among every race, culture, society and civilisation, permeating their literature, art, drama, music and myth.

All higher animals display jealous behaviour under appropriate conditions and humans exhibit such feelings within the first few months of life, after which the emotion never leaves us. Even the Almighty, it seems, admits to such feelings, since the second commandment cautions us not to worship any graven image: 'for I the Lord thy God am a jealous God, and visit the sins of the fathers upon the children unto the third and fourth generations.'

Before exploring the nature of jealousy in more detail, it is important to distinguish between jealousy and its close cousin *envy* with whom it shares the status of 'green-eyed monster' and with which it is frequently confused. The essential difference is that while envy arises from feelings of inequality between the envious and the envied, jealousy stems from assumptions either of equality or superiority. As Robert Solomon perceptively comments in his book *The Passions*: 'Unlike envy, jealousy wants the other to face its fabled green eye.'

While envy broods glowering from a distance, jealousy actively seeks out confrontation. While envy spreads itself diffusely, jealousy focuses precisely on some person, object, situation or circumstances of which the jealous person considers him, or herself, deprived. Indeed, this sense of deprivation is often the driving force behind the emotion.

'It is the claim of possession that is crucial,' stresses Solomon, 'not the importance of the object itself.'

Freud regarded jealousy as being compounded of a mixture of grief, resulting from the loss of a love object and its associated loss of self-esteem, of anger against a successful rival and of self-blame for having suffered such a loss.

This grief, rage and self-loathing come together to produce a force sufficiently powerful to subvert reason, banish caution and even override basic commonsense. In *Challenge to Survival*, anthropologist Leon Williams wrote that: 'Throughout history man has tried to protect himself and his society from the destructive effects of sexual jealousy.' All too often, it seems, to little or no good effect. Wars have been fought, countries laid waste, the innocent slain, feuds started and families destroyed as a direct result of this most powerful, complex and pervasive of emotions.

But is jealousy really as negatively destructive as most people seem to believe? Are writers justified in painting it as an emotion so dark and dangerous, as an unnatural, pathological response whose consequences will inevitably be harmful?

One of the earliest scientists to raise his voice in defence of jealousy was Charles Darwin, for whom it was no aberration but an essential element of the evolutionary process and, as such, a perfectly natural response which must, of necessity, enjoy universal expression. Jealousy, he believed, plays a key role in determining 'sexual selection', the tendency for certain 'fitter' animals to mate more often, and hence propagate their superior genes. It is jealousy, Darwin claimed, which drives a dominant male to secure, by all means available to him, sexual relations with one or more females.

Commenting on his observations of jealousy among mating geese, Konrad Lorenz observed that they provided a striking illustration of similar behaviours evolving independently in unrelated species. Lorenz wrote:

> The conclusion to be drawn from this . . . is as simple as it is important. Since we know that behaviour patterns of geese and men cannot possibly be homologous – the last common ancestors of birds and mammals were extremely primitive reptiles – with minute brains and certainly incapable of any complicated social behaviour – and since we know that the improbability of co-incidental similarity can only be expressed in astronomical numbers, we know for certain that it was more or less identical survival value which caused jealousy behaviour to evolve in birds as well as man.

He went on to make clear, however, that it was impossible to say either what the survival value might be, or to identify the physiological mechanisms which brought about jealousy in the two species.

> They may well be different in each case. Streamlining is achieved in the shark through the shape of the musculature, in the dolphin by means of a thick layer of blubber, and in the torpedo with welded steel plates.
> By the same token, jealousy may be – and probably is – caused by an inherited and genetically fixed program in geese, while it might be determined by cultural tradition in humans – though I do not think it is, at least not entirely.

Given the enormous range and complexity of human social exchanges, it is important to be able to recognise which behaviours originally possessed some survival value, even if that value has long since disappeared. In this way it is possible to distinguish between naturally occurring responses which, however bizarre and unhelpful their continuation in the modern world may be, cannot be considered pathological.

The chances for making such discoveries are, of course, greatly enhanced by discovering the same patterns of behaviour in an animal with which we can experiment.

Down through the centuries poets, novelists and playwrights have depicted the jealous man or woman as one seized by a kind of madness. There are, indeed, cases in which the jealousy reaches a level at which it can reasonably be said to be a form of insanity, and we will explore these cases in more detail a little later in this chapter. But, in general, it can be said that far from being an aberration, or a symptom of mankind's warped nature, jealousy is a natural response which carries with it important evolutionary advantages.

In the higher animals, jealousy takes on a far more human face as the observations on chimpanzees, made by Wolfgang Kohler, Professor of Philosophy at the University of Berlin revealed. Writing about their attitudes towards humans, Kohler noted that:

If one is specially friendly to, and plays more, with any one of the animals, the others not seldom become jealous. For instance, when Tercera saw anything like this, she would begin to walk about restlessly, looking at me, and after piteous and reproachful sounds, she would approach me and nudge me again and again, so as to turn my attention away from the other animal to her, or else, pouting all the time, would try to push the other animal away and take its place. I must say that sometimes Tercera's behaviour came pretty close to that of a coquette.

But even when a response is, at root, instinctive, human beings bring to that behaviour a vast array of learned behaviours which subtly change and modify the innate master-plan programmed into our genes. For this reason human and animal displays of jealousy are likely to be different both in style and form. And this holds true even when the other animal is a highly intelligent primate, as a remarkable study by Dr William Kellog has established.

Professor W. N. Kellog, associate professor of psychology at Indiana university, reared a chimpanzee, named Gua, in the company of his son who was the same age as the chimp. During their early years chimp and child were reared in much the same way, and both displayed jealousy on many occasions although it was never an especially significant response.

During the early months the little boy would laugh delightedly when an adult played with Gua, and never showed any signs of being jealous or of wanting to join in their game. As he grew older, however, his interest grew stronger and he would often go towards the activity. Sometimes, too, if Gua put her hands upon his walker or climbed onto his high chair he pushed her away. In his account of the experiment, Kellog reports that

> At the start . . . he permitted her to take things from him without objecting.
>
> By the time the child was 16 months of age they seemed each to want the same toys and would frequently tussle over a single play object like two squabbling children.
>
> As early as the eighth month Gua, for her part, would push Donald's hands from her walker when he reached out and grasped it, and she seemed to prefer the boy's walker to her own. She appeared similarly on many occasions to select the things with which he was playing, or had previously played, in preference to other toys. When Donald was spoken to or attended by others, Gua always rushed to the spot, and actively edged her way into the proceedings. If this could not be done by pushing herself between Donald and the person attending him, she would slap the legs of the latter, or even pull at Donald's clothing. Sometimes there was further evidence of jealous behaviour when one of her grown-up friends displayed affectionate behaviour to another without similarly noticing Gua at the same time. In such instances she would occasionally attack the recipient of the embraces with slaps and rarely with her teeth. And yet, in spite of such examples, Gua's jealousy was never very conspicuous or troublesome. Provided the two subjects were treated as any two children near the same age are treated, that is provided they were shown the same attention, and petted or talked to together, there was nothing striking or unusual in Gua's activity which would stamp her as radically different from a child in such situations. Her anger was never of an aggressive sort, nor did her jealousy appear to be so either, excepting in the affectionate situations mentioned.

The developmental aspects of jealousy were studied in a more conventional manner by Drs Steven Frankel, Professor of Psychiatry at the Children's Psychiatric Hospital, University of Michigan Medical Centre, and Ivan Sherick. Their aim was to look at the ways in which envy and jealousy were related and to discover at what point the first emotion gave way to the second, during the first five years of life. They were also interested to explore the part played by envy in regulating self-esteem.

From their study, Frankel and Sherick concluded that the emotions passed through a number of distinct stages of development linked to the child's chronological age.

STAGE 1   1 year or less
Here the child considers, and indeed treats, people and things as extensions or even parts of himself. She, or he, feels entitled to them and believes that they should be under their complete control. During this stage there seems to be little difference between jealousy and envy since the focus of attention is mainly other children's toys or games, although even at this early age a sense of possession did occasionally extend to other people. This suggests that both feelings arise from a common emotional source, although they quickly diverge.

At this stage of development, however, neither humans nor objects are recognised as possessing a separate identity and viewed solely in terms of their possession, a response which the researchers categorised as satisfying instinctual more than emotional needs.

STAGE 2   1.5–2 years
During this time the child grows increasingly interested in other people, and emotions as opposed to instincts play a larger role. They become valued in their own right, rather than purely in terms of the child's need, and this tends to increase the sense of frustration felt when the desired object is denied, leading to a more complex emotional reaction.

STAGE 3   2–3 years
At this stage, the child grows increasingly interested in other people as separate beings. The child's concern with possessions becomes more abstract and generalised. That is, he or she starts to covet not only physical objects such as toys and games belonging to another, but also starts reacting to less tangible possessions such as adult attention and recognition of other children or abilities and characteristics in another child which they believe lacking in themselves.

It is during this stage of development, therefore, that envy and jealousy appear to go their separate ways. At a point in mental growth when the child becomes capable of elaborating concepts away from the purely physical. This is also the time when children learn to delay their need for gratification, so decreasing their inclination to make an immediate grab for something they desire.

STAGE 4   3–4 years
According to the researchers, this is the time when girls start becoming jealous of boys and of their mothers. The most character-

istic need of children at this stage is to win the admiration of others, especially adults, and to possess anything that can help them in this quest. Jealousy is handled in a more adaptive and socially acceptable manner. Though they may still stridently demand the thing they want – or compete quite openly for the attentions of somebody whose admiration they desire, they are now capable of making polite requests and engaging in more considered, more mature, tactics to accomplish their goals.

STAGE 5   4–5 years

Here children use role-play to take on features of others of whom they are jealous. Jealousy, at this stage, may be expressed either directly, within a relationship, or indirectly through fantasy. Being ignored or neglected by others is a major source of concern and possibly the most important source of jealousy. Jealousy is especially noticeable in children who have been left out of games by their companions, especially when these peers are of the same sex. When the exclusion is by members of the opposite sex, boys of this age will generally try to keep girls from joining in their play, less jealousy is usually aroused. From the age of five onwards, therefore, jealousy wears a very adult face.

What this implies, especially in terms of very powerful feelings of jealousy, was spelled out in a detailed study by Robert Tipton and his colleagues at Virginia Commonwealth University in the United States. Adults were interviewed in depth about their jealous feelings and from these answers a 92 item 'jealousy' assessment was constructed. This was then administered to a large number of college students and the results analysed by computer.

In this way Tipton was able to identify five separate components of jealousy, each of which reflects some aspect of personality or temperament. An over-jealous man or woman appears to possess the following five characteristics.

First, they all have a great need for loyalty from those close to them, combined with a powerful desire for intimate relationships. They tend to be moodier than most, lack self-confidence and are inclined to envy the possessions, accomplishments, abilities and aptitudes of other people. When these emotions are both intense and experienced in a culture which regards them as not only acceptable but, under certain circumstances both desirable and honourable, the seeds are sown for the violent passions aroused by sexual jealousy, and most often seen among Southern males, especially those from Mediterranean countries.

In Italy, for example, the jealous rage of a man whose wife has been unfaithful to him not infrequently leads to murder. Indeed, the most serious insult one man can utter is to call another '*cornuto*' (cuckold), either verbally or non-verbally by extending the fore-finger and little finger vertically while curling the other fingers into the palm, so making the sign of a goat's horns, a token symbolically worn by the injured party. As tourists have sometimes discovered to their dismay, either of these two forms of insult is almost certain to result in a furious assault. If the police become involved, however, little action is likely to be taken since the attack is generally held to be a perfectly honourable response to extreme provocation.

This reaction naturally presents problems when one Italian male feels the need to inform his best friend of a wife's betrayal. He cannot simply tell him to his face since, even if they are the closest of friends, custom dictates that the insulted husband must regard the well-intended warning as a vicious assault on his honour and demand satisfaction via a duel with daggers. In order to break such news, therefore, a curious ritual has grown up in some parts of rural Italy. The informer waits until the wife is with her lover, then hides in an upstairs room overlooking the street down which he knows his friend is going to pass. At the appropriate moment, the informer, taking great care to remain concealed, shouts '*cornu-u-u-to*' through the open window. Tradition now demands that the husband appear outraged and immediately, but not very thoroughly, search for the man who has so insulted him. After devoting as little time as possible to the task, he can then hurry home to catch his wife and her lover in the act. The customary revenge exacted by the betrayed husband upon his wife and the lover is that of death. In such cases the courts sometimes take a relatively lenient view of such crimes, certainly seeing them as much less reprehensible than killing under almost any other circumstances.

In America, too, exceptions used to be made for murders mo-tivated by jealous rage. Although never formally codified there existed, until fairly recently, a tacit understanding, lawyers dubbed it an 'unwritten law', between the defence attorney and the judge when a defendant caught his wife and her lover fornicating, he could not be held responsible for his actions. Provided that the slaying was carried out directly, while the man was possessed of a jealous fury, the court tended to be extremely lenient.

Throughout the early part of the twentieth century, a vast number of husbands who killed their wives and, or, the lover were either acquitted or given only token sentences under this 'unwritten law'. The usual practice was for the husband to plead 'temporary insan-ity', a defence almost invariably viewed with favour by the courts.

Interestingly, however, jealous women who murdered their husbands in the heat of passion fared less well, and frequently discovered that pleas of 'temporary insanity' were not sufficient to save them from prison. Today, however, a defence based on this plea is unlikely to assist defendants of either sex.

In some cultures it is more advantageous for the man to make the breakup of his marriage due to a wife's adultery as public a display as possible. Among the Hidatsa Indians of North America, for instance, while it is permissible to kill the unfaithful wife, opinion holds that a far more admirable response is to make an elaborate display of presenting her to his rival. Considered even more laudable is the husband who throws in a few of his possessions, along with the wife, in a shammed attempt to get him to take her off his hands.

Even in those societies where sexual attitudes are more relaxed and crimes of passion far less acceptable, infidelity is becoming an increasingly important cause of marital break-up. A 1952 survey, carried out in the UK by National Marriage Guidance Council, found that only 8% cited their partner's unfaithfulness as a main problem, sexual difficulties were mentioned by 18%, and money by 2.5%. Twenty-five years later, when the survey was repeated, all these figures had risen. Money was now a source of dissatisfaction among 8% of couples, while sex was a problem for 31%. Infidelity, however, had seen the largest rise of all, up 14% to 22%. In America it appears to be an ever more common cause of break-up, with 51% of males interviewed by the sexologist Alfred Kinsey giving it as the main reason for seeking a divorce.

Although jealousy is a psychological phenomenon which is 'at least as common as chicken-pox', according to American behavioural scientist Dr Jeff Bryson, surprisingly few in-depth studies of it appear in the psychological literature.

In this respect it shares much in common with loneliness. Psychologists adopting a scientific approach to the study of behaviour tend to shy away from both topics because they are so difficult to define precisely, so broad-based and so diffuse. An exception to this general rule is Dr Bryson, who was interested in establishing the extent to which the physical attractiveness of a third party in a love triangle would affect the degree of jealousy aroused.

His approach, which brought a touch of television soap opera into the unlikely surroundings of the psychological laboratory, was to write a script, hire professional actors, and turn film director to create short video-tapes depicting somewhat trite but fairly typical jealousy-arousing scenarios.

His film opened with the camera panning slowly across a relaxed party scene, before coming to rest on a couple sitting on the sofa, cuddling and kissing. After a while one of them got up and went off to fetch some drinks. Soon afterwards another guest joined the first on the couch and took up the romantic action. The predictable ending was the return of the original partner and his or her outraged reactions.

The film was shot using different actors so that in one version the interloper was played by a very attractive person, while in the other he or she appeared as unattractive as possible. The two scenes were then shown to an audience of male and female students who were asked to complete a questionnaire after all the films had been shown. On this they had to report their own likely response, in the same situation, by rating the intensity of 36 different emotions.

Dr Bryson quickly found that men differed significantly in their stated response to the situation, saying that they would seek their revenge by going out with other women or by becoming sexually aggressive towards them.

Women, however, were more likely to put on a show of indifference and attempt to ignore what had happened. They also said they would take positive action to preserve the relationship by making themselves more attractive to their philandering boy-friends.

Women also differed from men in their immediate emotional response to the slight, remaining outwardly cool in public but giving way to tears when alone. Men, on the other hand, were more likely to make a public display of their emotions by threatening the interloper or getting drunk. Strangely, however, they also reported being perversely flattered by the attentions of the interloper and to feel even more turned on by their partner.

These differences were especially marked when the interloper was played by an attractive actor or actress. The males' response to abandon the relationship then became more prevalent, while the females were more likely to make themselves even more appealing and to attempt to patch things up.

Dr Bryson believes that these reactions can be explained by the traditional roles and power-plays which society assigns to men and women in heterosexual relationships. Society, he points out, expects men to initiate relationships, take an active role in maintaining them, and to be the more assertive of the two.

This pattern of response to jealousy-arousing events, the male's tendency to sever and the female's to persevere is, of course, a long-established tradition in romantic fiction and popular music, especially among writers of Country and Western lyrics. In Hank Williams' song, 'Your Cheatin' Heart', for example, a wronged male – unconditionally deserting the unfaithful woman in his life – tells her in no uncertain terms how, even in the dead of night, she will dearly regret his leaving.

94

> . . . you'll toss and turn
> and call my name.
> But sleep won't come
> the whole night through.
> Your cheatin' heart
> will tell on you.

The female response to betrayal, that is to attempt to save a threatened relationship, is typified by the lyric of the song 'Jolene' in which the wronged wife seeks out her more attractive rival and begs her . . .

> Jolene, Jolene, Jolene
> please don't take my man.
> . . . even if you can.

Deliberately seeking to arouse jealousy in a partner is, of course, a form of love-play as old as romance itself, but recent research has found that the reasons for this manoeuvre and the means by which it is carried out, vary markedly between men and women.

Dr Gregory White of the University of Maryland developed a 'Relationships Questionnaire' designed to provide detailed insight into the workings of romantic attachments. This included such questions as, 'Have you ever tried to get your partner jealous on purpose?' 'Who would you say is more involved in your relationship, you or your partner?'

When he reviewed the answers provided by dating couples, Dr White discovered that deliberate attempts to make the partner jealous were extremely common and that techniques for doing so included openly flirting with a third person in the presence of one's sex partner, dating somebody else, inventing another attachment, and openly discussing a former relationship in one partner's presence.

A statistical analysis of the subject's responses revealed that women, while in the company of their partners, pretended to get interested in, and openly to flirt with, members of the opposite sex more frequently than did their partners, although a significant proportion of men confessed to using this tactic. However the reasons for wanting to make their partner jealous were different. While 38% of females said that they tried to make the man in their life jealous in order to gain some sort of reward, such as more attention and interest, this motive was present in only 15% of males.

The commonest motive given by both sexes, however, was 'to see if he/she still cares'.

Among the women in Dr White's study, the degree of involvement with their partner was highly correlated with the amount of jealousy aroused. Women who said that they were deeply involved with their partner were almost twice as likely to try and make him feel jealous. No such relationship was found among the men. Such jealousy-provoking behaviour seems especially paradoxical in the light of Jeff Bryson's findings. For, as his study showed, when a women makes her partner jealous she runs a serious risk of losing him. Even devoted partners are most likely to respond to such provocation by ending the relationship. Similarly, the marked tendency for women who are deeply involved in a relationship to try and make their partner jealous is equally curious, since they presumably place greater importance on it than the less involved.

Once jealousy has taken root, part of its especially destructive power seems to stem from the fact that marked social disapproval inhibits free discussion of the problem among those whose relationship is threatened. People simply don't want to talk about such feelings, not to their friends or relatives and especially not to the jealousy-provoking partner.

When Janice Francis of Purdue University explored this aspect of jealousy, using questionnaires and interviews, she found that even when such problems were seemingly resolved, they frequently simmered away below the surface, slowly but surely corroding the relationship.

This leads them to be over-concerned with how other people behave, although their reaction is usually to confront threatening situations head-on rather than seek to escape them through some sort of avoidance strategy.

Bringle and Williams found that most over-jealous men and women come into the category of 'non-screeners' and strong 'sensitizers', in other words they find it hard to distinguish between relevant and irrelevant information in their surroundings and have a very low threshold for emotionally charged information. In addition they have above average anxiety and tend to respond obsessionally or to try and intellectualise away their feelings. The same researchers have also found that people who are excessively jealous generally think rather badly of themselves, feel less satisfied with their life than most, are prone to depression and more malevolent in their dealings with the world.

Bringle also found that such individuals are more likely to possess what psychologists define as an 'external locus of control', which means that they seek explanations for life's ups and downs in the world around them, rather than reflecting on the contribution of their own attitudes and behaviours to the things which happen to them. This leads them to blame their misfortunes on bad luck or on the faults and failings of others.

What, then, is the final portrait which emerges of an excessively jealous individual?

First, once the notion that they have some cause to be jealous takes possession of them, they are likely to be extremely selective in the search for evidence to support this belief. Their lack of screening ability leads them to focus attention on irrelevant, but emotionally arousing, information while overlooking or ignoring facts that point to an alternative explanation. When Iago feeds Othello's suspicions about Desdemona's infidelity, by asking whether she ever owned a handkerchief 'spotted with strawberries', and remarking that 'such a handkerchief, I am sure it was your wife's – did I today see Cassio wipe his beard with', Othello immediately accepts his assertion that 'It speaks against her . . .' and this becomes, to his distorted vision, clear evidence of his wife's unfaithfulness, and a focus for his obsessive ruminations. As Iago's wife, Emily, so aptly puts it: 'Jealous souls will not be answered so. They are not ever jealous for the cause, but jealous for they are jealous: 'tis a monster begot upon itself . . .'

Lacking in self-esteem, and seeing himself, or herself, the victim of life rather than capable of exerting control over events, the over-jealous brood on their misfortune and then confront those held to be responsible for betraying them head-on in outbursts of fury, or through sullen discontent.

Jealousy, then, is an inborn response whose evolutionary purpose was to enhance the fitness of a species. An immensely complex emotional response, which has developed in humans by the age of five, it can be used as a deliberate strategy – although a far from satisfactory one – in love-play. It can also become a force powerful enough to destroy relationships entirely.

According to Freud's view, of course, the first relationship at risk is that between infant and parent when the male child's love for his mother results in the growth of a jealous hatred for his father, the well-known Oedipus Complex. In the next chapter we will be exploring these aspects of psychosexual development to discover what influence such childhood feelings may exert on personal attraction in adult life.

7

The myths of mother love

Don't poets know,
Better than others?
God can't always be everywhere: and so,
Invented Mothers.

Sir Edwin Arnold
Mothers.

A few years ago an unfortunate error, by staff in the busy maternity ward of an Israeli hospital, resulted in several mothers taking the wrong baby back home. A fortnight later, when embarrassed doctors contacted the families to explain the mix-up and put matters right, they were astonished to find a reluctance on the part of many women to give up a stranger's child. While all the fathers were eager to recover their own infant, a majority of their wives asked to be allowed to carry on raising another woman's baby.

This surprising response provides an excellent illustration of the powerful mechanisms that form the biological basis for mother love; the bonding process which occurs within the first few moments after birth. Once formed, this bond, a kind of genetic superglue, creates a union between the woman and her child which influences their response to one another for ever after. It is a bond so potent that, as the Israeli story shows, it can even triumph over what many would regard as the mother's 'natural' desire to raise her own, rather than somebody else's, flesh and blood.

In this chapter we shall be exploring the biology of this process and seeing what happens when, for a variety of reasons, bonding fails to take place. We shall also consider the historical and cultural aspects of this unique human relationship, since it is only by understanding the pressure these exert on personal and social perceptions and expectations that one can appreciate the enormous influence exerted by the five myths of mother love.

Myth number one states that all mothers must love and naturally desire to nurture their children.

Myth two, which follows from the first, claims that mothers who do not love or wish to nurture their offspring are abnormal to the point of wickedness.

Myth three, again a natural progression from the assumptions of the first two myths, maintains that the natural mother is always the best person to bring up a child.

Myth four tells us that, since only women are capable of fulfilling this role, motherhood is their primary social function.

Finally there is the myth which asserts that children will naturally love their mother (and father) and that not to do so is either perverse, or pathological, or both.

As you will realise these myths exert a very profound influence over our attitudes towards the relationship between mother and child, both as sons or daughters, as mothers or fathers, and as members of a culture which places such a premium on this kind of loving.

Before we consider these consequences in detail, let's explore both the biology and sociology of a mother's love. We'll begin, where life itself starts, in the delivery room immediately after the child has been born. For it is during these vital minutes, many experts believe, that the foundations of love are laid down.

THE BIOLOGY OF BONDING

That such a basic, primitive and powerful mechanism as biological bonding exists in many animal species is beyond doubt. For most mammals there is a critical period, which may last for no more than a few minutes, during which bonding has to occur before the mother recognises and is prepared to raise the youngster as her own. A young goat removed from the nanny for just five minutes after birth, for example, will be firmly rejected thereafter.

Once bonding has occurred, mother and offspring respond to one another with behaviours more compelling and insistent than are expressed at any other time, with the possible exception of sexual arousal. One of the most important and powerful of these is *imprinting*, a word taken from the German *Pragnung* which means coining or stamping. It was first applied by ethologists in Germany to the habit of newly hatched ducks or geese of automatically following their mother wherever she goes. So rigid and compulsive is this behaviour that they can be persuaded to follow any moving object that is presented to them in the critical period following their hatching.

This remarkable fact was first demonstrated by the great ethologist Konrad Lorenz who raised geese on his large estates near Vienna. He observed that newly hatched goslings followed their mother wherever she went. However, when he took them from the mother and raised them in an incubator, they could be easily be misled into believing that Lorenz himself was their mother and would then follow him instead.

Before long his neighbours became quite used to seeing Konrad Lorenz taking strolls around the countryside followed obediently by half a dozen goslings. Later work showed that the baby birds could also be fooled into trailing after wood models of geese, and even footballs, cardboard boxes and model trains.

The obvious question is how much this kind of behaviour tells us about the response between a human mother and her infant. To what extent is imprinting important in the formation of a bond between the two and what will happen if something occurs to prevent that bond from being formed.

Devising experiments that might provide an answer would, of course, be cruel and highly unethical. But some clues are provided by studying such behaviour in our closest cousins in the animal kingdom, the primates. Anthropologist Dr Desmond Morris, for example, argues that because we are closely related to certain species of monkey, much of our behaviour, including imprinting, forms part of a common heritage.

One of the researchers who has approached the problem through work with primates is Dr Harry Harlow, who carried out a famous series of experiments in which baby monkeys removed from their natural mothers shortly after birth were raised by one of two artificial surrogates. Both consisted of wire frames and had wooden heads; either could be rigged to dispense milk on demand. But the critical difference between them was that while the wire frame of one remained uncovered, the other was made soft and cuddly through the use of foam rubber and terry-cloth. He found that it was not the dispensing of food which mattered to the motherless infants but the softness of the surrogate's body. When given the choice all the infants would spend most of their time clinging to the terry cloth covered frame while the bare frame, even when it alone offered food, was ignored.

Not only was the soft mother more comforting, it also seemed to provide the baby with a greater sense of security. When an unfamiliar object was introduced into the cage, infants without a soft surrogate tended to be fearful and to ignore it. But if they had the comfort of the terry-cloth substitute they were far bolder and would approach and touch the object provided they could remaining attached to the 'mother' by one hand.

In later experiments, Harlow explored other features which made the surrogate more acceptable. He found, for instance, that baby monkeys preferred a fake mother who rocked backwards and forwards. Body temperature too was important, with the baby preferring an electrically heated wire frame to one merely covered with foam and terry-cloth.

But while feeding and protection are important elements of successful caring, providing a sense of security is no less critical. Infant monkeys who were raised in varying degrees of isolation during their early months showed various kinds of social incompetence and some even behaved in a pathological way as adults. When kept isolated for six months, for instance, they were aberrant in almost every respect when fully grown, being incapable of playing, defending themselves against attacks from others or engaging in sexual activities. His conclusion was that early social deprivation permanently impairs a monkey's ability to have effective relations with others.

Close bonding to the mother shortly after birth seems, therefore, to be a vital factor in successful emotional development.

Konrad Lorenz was one of the first scientists to appreciate that the shape of a baby is a vital factor in triggering maternal – and to a lesser extent paternal – responses in all kinds of animals. He labelled this signal a 'releaser' because its effect is to release a complex series of feelings and behaviours which help ensure adequate rearing.

The releaser operates at a very basic, biological level and is primarily an inborn response, although learning and experience, especially in humans, has an important role to play in shaping this primitive reaction. Some of the earliest investigations into the way that this 'releaser' operates was carried out in the Fifties by Dr M. A. Cann of the University of Chicago. He had an artist produce drawings of more than 50 kinds of animals, including humans, in both infant and adult state. These pictures were then shown to a wide cross-section of the population, married and single women and men, couples with children and childless, young adults, middle-aged people and the elderly. Each was asked to state a preference for either the infant or adult drawing and invited to explain their choice.

Dr Cann found that all the women revealed a marked preference for drawings of young animals, but the intensity of that interest differed depending on whether they were single or married, had children or were childless. The liking for baby pictures increased according to marital status and whether or not they had a family of their own.

Where males were concerned, although there was less bias in favour of pictures of the young, those who were married and had children of their own generally showed a greater preference than bachelors or married men without children of their own.

A decade later a more sophisticated variation of this basic idea was carried out by Dr Eckhard Hess, following a fascinating scientific discovery which he had made in the least probable of circumstances – while reading beside his wife, in bed.

Absorbed in a book of animal studies, Dr Hess was startled when his wife, who had been watching him closely for a while remarked that she could tell whenever he was looking at a picture of special interest because the pupils of his eyes enlarged.

As is well known, the iris of the eye acts like the aperture of a camera and controls the amount of light entering. If we come in from a brightly lit garden, where the pupil will be small, into a dull room it will automatically open out in order to allow more light to fall on the retina. But, as Mrs Hess had noticed, the pupil also dilates whenever we are aroused or attracted by something. As with the light reflex, this movement is entirely automatic and controlled by a part of the nervous system over which we do not, normally, have any direct control.

Interestingly this unconscious dilation of the pupils has an important, but seldom recognised, part to play in mutual attraction. When we sight somebody who arouses our interest, the automatic widening of our pupils signals this fact to them. When the attraction is mutual, so too is the dilation and this tends to intensify those feelings.

When psychologists presented males with seemingly identical photographs of a girl's face and asked them to pick the one which seemed most attractive, a majority selected just one of the two snaps. Unknown to them an artist had subtly retouched the pupils, making them larger on one picture and smaller on another. This directed their liking towards the photograph in which the pupils had been enlarged because, although none of the subjects realised it, they were responding to an apparent signal of attraction in the girl's eyes.

Hess used this finding to measure the level of arousal produced by photographs of various kinds. In order to record changes in pupil size accurately, he photographed the eyes of volunteers using invisible infra-red light and then carefully measured the photographs. His results confirmed the findings of earlier studies. Interest in pictures of human babies and young animals varied according to the viewers' sex, marital status and their involvement with children.

But what is it that makes these images so appealing?

If you reflect on the shape of young animals, you'll quickly see that they have certain characteristics in common. Infants are not merely smaller versions of grown-ups, they possess unique, physical features. Their limbs, for instance, are short and heavy, their stomachs bulge, and – most strikingly of all – their head is out of proportion to their body. They have plump cheeks, large foreheads and prominent eyes, which due to the size of the forehead may be located towards the middle of their face.

It is these specific characteristics which, many believe, serve to release important emotional responses and biologically programmed behaviours in adult animals. Kittens, puppies, lion cubs, foals, lambs and calves, for example, generate very different reactions among humans from those aroused by cats, dogs, lions, horses, sheep and cattle. We tend to think of them as 'cute' and 'cuddly' and to feel protective towards them. Cruelty to a kitten or puppy, for instance, is usually regarded as a far more heinous crime than the ill-treatment of grown-up animals. Many human babies too suffer from their mother's desire to emphasise these 'babyish' features through over-feeding. However much experts warn against stuffing babies, a significant number of mothers still regard a chubby child as more attractive than a thinner one in whom the releaser features are less apparent.

There is, indeed, evidence to suggest that children lacking such natural releasers, who are less able to trigger the caretaking instinct in adults, may suffer serious consequences. Social workers sometimes find children who are repeatedly neglected or ill-treated and for whom even warm and caring foster families can raise little enthusiasm. In one tragic case a thin, somewhat 'unbabylike' infant was removed from his natural parents after being battered and placed with foster parents. Although this couple had looked after other babies with great care and tenderness it was not long before the horrified case-worker realised that the child was being abused by his new parents. Transferred to yet another carefully selected family it was not long before the baby was again being battered.

Probably the most successful commercial exploiter of biological releasers was Walt Disney who was clever enough to design the characters of all his heroes and heroines in such a way that they incorporated these basic biological triggers for appeal – large heads and stubby limbs, big eyes and heads out of proportion to their body. His villains, by comparison, are all thin and scrawny and so unable to trigger off feelings of warmth and caring love.

Disney couldn't have known about biological releasers when Micky Mouse (called Mortimer Mouse in those early days) first appeared on the cinema screens in 1928. Presumably Disney was just either lucky or highly intuitive when he drew the mouse as he did.

Certainly its powerful biological triggers were crucial in establishing Micky as one of the screens all-time, international stars. Nor is all this mere speculation, for work by Dr Hess has confirmed that the closer animals are drawn to correspond with the Disney ideal, the greater the pupil dilation – and therefore the stronger the subconscious arousal and interest – they produce.

It seems likely that not only is the shape of the baby a crucial factor, but the act of childbirth itself may also serve as a trigger for biologically programmed responses.

Even doctors and midwives who have been present at hundreds of childbirths report that each is special to them, and husbands who have watched their child born usually report that they found it a significant and profoundly moving experience.

Such powerful feelings can even affect objective researchers, as delegates to a symposium on parent–infant relations discovered after they had watched a film of childbirth. One doctor commented on the infectious excitement which had spread through the audience, and many others agreed. Expressing the general view, Dr Bentovim of the Hospital for Sick Children in London, commented that: 'The boundaries between each of us seemed to dissolve with the shared feeling. The potential for ecstasy therefore seems to be universally present, particularly in those with a vested interest in infancy.'

Sight, sounds and – as we have already seen – odours are key elements in the biology of bonding. But so too is touch, that most neglected of our senses. For it is through touching, stroking, caressing and cuddling that the mother sends her own messages of comfort and reassurance to her newly born infant.

A detailed study carried out by Dr M. H. Klaus, of the Department of Pediatrics of America's Case Western Reserve University, has shown that while all mothers caress their infants in generally the same way, there are small – but vital – differences in the way this touching occurs, depending on the period which elapsed between the birth and the mother being able to have close contact with her baby.

Dr Klaus reports that: 'The same sequence of behaviour was observed in all the mothers of full-term infants when they first interacted with them. Every woman began with fingertip-touching on the infant's extremities and proceeded within the first four to eight minutes to massaging and encompassing palm contact on the trunk.'

First the mother would gently and soothingly touch the fingers, hands and toes of her baby with her own fingertips. Then she began stroking the child's face and body. After a few moments she used her whole hand, massaging with her palm. As she did so the mother became increasingly excited and then more and more relaxed.

For this sequence to be followed, however, certain physical conditions were necessary. The child had to be naked and there had to be privacy. In an earlier series of observations, during which the babies had been kept wrapped in a blanket, it needed many more sessions before fingertip caresses changed to the full hand massage. The presence of strangers also disrupted the pattern of touch.

Mothers who had their babies at home showed a slightly different sequence of caresses, which started with stroking of the baby's face before quickly switching to the full-palm massage. Not only was face- and body-touching begun far more rapidly, but there was also more overall contact during early sessions. Dr Klaus believes that these differences can be explained by the fact that home-delivered children are usually given to the mother far earlier than those born in a busy hospital. He also comments that: 'In sharp contrast to the woman who gives birth in hospital, the woman who delivers at her own home appears to be in control of the process. She chooses the room in the house and the location within the room for her birth, as well as guests who will be present. She is an active participant during her labour and delivery rather than a passive patient.'

While it would be wrong to assume that home confinement is always superior to a hospital delivery, there is evidence that modern childbirth practices can interefere with the bonding process in ways which may have unrealised significance for the future relationship.

In a special study carried out by three American doctors, John Kennell, Mary Anne Trause and Marshall Klaus, all from the Case Western Reserve University, the nature and extent of this early bonding between mother and child has been put under the microscope. The 28 mothers-to-be who volunteered to take part in the study were randomly allocated to one of two groups. The first received normal treatment provided for mothers in the maternity departments of North American hospitals.

They were allowed a brief glimpse of the baby immediately after birth, a further short period of contact some six to eight hours later, and visits of around 30 minutes for feeding, every four hours. The second group was able to hold and caress their nude babies for an hour after birth and for an additonal five hours each day during the next three days.

In a similar study carried out at Guatemala's Roosevelt Hospital, some mothers were given their naked babies immediately on leaving the delivery-room while others, again in line with normal hospital routine, did not see them for 12 hours after birth.

The results from both these experiments were clear-cut and convincing. Early contact led to far more caresses, and to a closer relationship which involved more fondling, clasping, holding, massaging and intensity of gaze.

But the routine separation of mother and child are not the only ways in which present-day medical practice may interfere with the spontaneous development of a relationship between mother and baby. During a conference on parents and children, Dr John Kennell warned his colleagues that drastic things were done in the name of good hospital practice: 'We put solutions in the baby's eyes that blur his vision and cause swelling of the lids, which sometimes closes the eyes. We wash and wipe the baby's skin and the mother's nipples, which probably changes the odours. Our procedures interfere with many parts of the mother's specific behaviour with her baby at this particular time. These interferences as well as the separation may drastically disturb the attachment process. The mother is given drugs that dull her perceptions and cause amnesia during a period when heightened responsiveness may be needed for attachment to occur.'

But how much does this matter to the child's development and the formation of a healthy bond between them?

Certainly imprinting is critical in some animals, as we have seen a separation of even a few minutes can lead to lasting rejection of the offspring. But human beings are not genetically programmed in this rigid way and can use reasoning and emotional responses of far greater complexity and flexibility to overcome initial set-backs and partings. Premature infants who must spend days or weeks in an incubator with little or no contact between them and their mothers are not necessarily going to be loved any less than those born under biologically ideal, early-contact conditions. That having been said, the evidence does seem to show that early contact with as little interference as possible in the natural process of childbirth is desirable and can yield beneficial results.

Early-contact mothers in both the North American and Guatemalan study did respond differently to their children later in life. Those from the Case Western study who had received 16 hours extra contact tended to relate more strongly to their children during later visits to the hospital. They stood close to them, held them more and gave greater eye contact. Similarly, physicians who saw early contact mothers in the Guatemalan hospital found no difficulty in identifying them on subsequent visits because their behaviour towards the growing child seemed so much warmer. Clearly touching and holding the infant had become a natural and spontaneous reaction.

There is also evidence to suggest that the warmth and security provided by such close bonding can exert a profound influence over the child's development. In a study of the effects of physical contact on intellectual growth, Dr Matas and his colleagues presented a series of problems, which required the use of tools, to 2-year-olds. He found that when the child felt insecure, due to a poor relationship, the likely response to setbacks in working out a solution was anger and frustration. They gave up easily, refused to ask for assistance and even rejected helpful advice from adults.

Children in secure relationships with their parents, on the other hand, were more likely to persevere and keep their cool if things didn't go right. They sought out and made good use of advice from adults and so solved the problems more rapidly and more successfully.

Personality too appears to be influenced by early bonding, as an investigation by another American researcher, Dr Waters, has shown. He found that secure children showed greater qualities of leadership, were more likely to initiate games or make the first move to gain co-operation from others in solving a group problem.

Some may feel that, despite my remarks on the flexibility of our responses, as compared with other animals, any suggestion that the basis of mother love is biological is demeaning to the human spirit, placing us on a level with the beasts in the field and carrying with it the assumption that without some strong biological bonding human mothers would neglect or abuse their offspring. The history of childhood, however, suggests that far from being able to rely on the milk of human kindness to ensure that infants survived and flourished, the newborn of earlier generations needed all the help biology could provide.

THE UNSPARED ROD

While, today it may seem only natural that mothers should love their children and be loved in return, a study of family life in the past reveals that even the bond of biology did not prevent parents from treating children in ways which were not merely cruel but on many occasions fatal. As Professor Edward Shorter shows in his book *The Making of the Modern Family*, even in recent times mothers were often indifferent to the health, the happiness and even the very survival of their infants. Neglect and ill-treatment were all too often the fate of the under-fives, a destiny from which neither wealth nor nobility of birth afforded protection.

The rich in their castles were just as likely to beat, brutalise, starve and even murder their infants as the poor in their hovels. In France an infant brother of Henri IV fell several stories to his death during a macabre game of catch, in which courtiers laughingly tossed the swaddled baby from one palace window to the next. Somebody missed and the screaming infant plunged to the cobbled yard below. Nor was this grisly scene all that unusual, since these 'games' were one of the ways in which European courtiers fairly often entertained themselves.

Swaddling too was widely practised, not out of any desire to be unkind but, on the contrary, because such tight binding was looked on as essential to the baby's survival. Without restraints it was feared that they might scratch out their eyes, break arms or legs, pull off their ears, deform their bones or crawl like an animal on all fours.

In 1826 a American doctor named William Dewees published his *Treatise on the Physical and Medical Treatment of Children*, which provides us with a detailed description of how and why this barbaric process was carried out.

Dewees comments that although it took up to two hours to swaddle the baby, nurses or parents usually considered the time well-spent since, once bound up like an Egyptian mummy, the wretched infant could, thereafter, be completely ignored.

Traditional swaddling, Dewees explained, 'consists in entirely depriving the child of the use of its limbs, by enveloping them in an endless length bandage, so as to not unaptly resemble billets of wood; and by which, the skin is sometimes excoriated; the flesh compressed, almost to gangrene; the circulation nearly arrested; and the child without the slightest power of motion. Its little waist is surrounded by stays . . . its head is compressed into the form the fancy of the midwife might suggest; and its shape maintained by properly adjusted pressure.'

No less cruel a practice, and one which was widely adopted by upper and middle-class European mothers was the employment of wet-nurses to suckle their infants, since women looked on the prospect of breast-feeding their babies with abhorrence. So widespread were these feelings that, late into the eighteenth century, mothers who were too poor to employ a wet nurse preferred feeding their babies on pap rather than allow them to suckle.

This use of wet nurses persisted despite the fact that those left in their care were far more likely to die in infancy than children raised by their own mothers at home.

Indeed the high infant mortality rate seems to have been regarded as regrettable but inevitable, as a passage in the autobiography of one nobleman, Sir Simonds D'Ewes, makes clear. His baby, like so many others, perished from ill-treatment and neglect after being farmed out to a 'a poor woman who had been much misused and almost starved by a wicked husband, being herself also naturally of a proud, fretting and wayward disposition: which together in the issue conducted to the final ruin and destruction of our most sweet and tender infant.'

The rector of one rural British parish described how when he first came to the area it was filled with 'suckling infants from London'. Within a year he had buried all but two of them.

Despite the loss of life, wet-nursing disappeared only slowly. In England and America it continued into the eighteenth century, in France to the nineteenth, while in Germany infants were still being sent away from home in the early part of the twentieth century.

Those who survived returned, often as late as the age of five, to homes where brutality appears to have been the rule rather than the exception. In his *History of Childhood*, Lloyd Demause notes that out of 200 statements of advice about child-rearing published before the eighteenth century, all but three advocated child-beating in certain circumstances and most approved of severe floggings. A further study of the lives of 70 children yielded only one example of a child raised without recourse to the rod.

He reports that 'Beating instruments included whips of all kinds, including the cat-o'-nine-tails, shovels, canes, iron and wooden rods, bundles of sticks, the *discipline* (a whip made of small chains), and special school instruments like the flapper, which had a pear-shaped end and a round hole to raise blisters.'

The use of such instruments was frequent and wide-spread. A German schoolmaster estimated that during his career he had administered 911,527 strokes with the stick, 124,000 lashes with the whip, 136,715 slaps with the hand, and 1,115,800 boxes on the ear.

From royal courts to rustic cottages the swish of the cane and crack of the whip would seem to have been the most persistent sounds of childhood. Beethoven beat his pupils with knitting needles and occasionally bit them. Milton's wife was shocked by the cries of her husband's nephews as he flogged them. Louis XII of France was beaten from 17 months onwards, by his father who kept a whip beside him at table. From the age of two beatings were regular and severe. He was even whipped on the day of his coronation at the age of eight, and as an adult still awoke in terror from nightmares about an expected whipping the following day.

Nor were fathers sole wielders of the whip while mothers remained silent but accepting. Writing of her early struggles with a four-month old child, one mother described how she whipped him 'until he was black and blue, and until I could not whip him any more, and he never gave up one single inch.' Horrific as this account may appear it is far from rare, nor – as we shall see in a moment – are the graphic descriptions of such savage acts the product of a bygone and more brutal age.

Even when they were not beating children themselves, many mothers either encouraged masters to flog them at school or accepted the most appalling treatment of their offspring by others with apparent equanimity. In his history of the British public school, John Chandos describes how one mother complained bitterly when a master refused to beat her son, saying that she had sent him to Eton to be flogged. Others turned a blind eye to pleas for help from their incarcerated children.

When 15-year-old Etonian, Pierce Taylor, wrote of horrendous beatings in a letter to his mother: 'If a boy missed a word (when repeating Homer) I will not say he whipped them, but he butchered them, he cut one of the boys so who was with me that he was quite raw, and he had got his lessons as well as he could I am certain.' No voice was raised in protest.

Indeed, Chandos refers to a letter from another mother apologising for her son's delayed return to school and explaining that he had not yet recovered from beatings received during the previous term. Small wonder then that Lloyd Demause describes childhood as 'a nightmare from which we have only recently begun to awaken'.

The extent of that awakening seems at times in question, for many mothers still find little difficulty in reconciling expressions of deep love towards their children with the infliction of pain, humiliation and distress.

'Up to the present I have been chastising my 3 daughters by spanking them with my hand after taking their knickers down, but this has no effect at all. The two younger ones aged 10 and 12 are both untidy and disobedient whilst the oldest who is nearly 16 is also insolent and I am very sorry to say deceitful.'

This letter, one of many on the same theme, appeared not in some pornographic magazine but in a middle-class, privately printed newsletter called *Family View*, a journal whose respectable readers are – according to the editor – parents possessing both 'sense and humour'.

Family View emphasises such 'traditional' values as discipline in the home and law and order in the streets. In a pamphlet, entitled 'Parents who cane . . . care', from the same publishers, a writer voices the opinion that: 'Punishing children is distasteful to all parents and teachers, but many (we believe the majority) find that chastising in some way is necessary and beneficial to the child.' He then goes on to provide useful hints for keeping canes in good condition (standing the stem in tepid water keeps it pliable); safeguarding the instrument of punishment (purchase two canes, one for show the other safely locked away in case the child destroys the one on view); and administering the punishment (never on the hand, 'six of the best is usually sufficient', 'pants afford the modesty a child is entitled to'.)

This last piece of advice appears to have passed by many of the correspondents to *Family View* who stress the importance of nudity when beating their children.

'My daughter's bottom glowed like a cigarette in the dark', enthused one satisfied mother after employing a leather spanking paddle marketed through the magazine and advertised as especially suitable for children under the age of 15.

Another well-pleased customer explained that she had used one when beating both her daughters: 'The 15-year-old was the first to get it, when I found cigarettes in her school bag and gave her 20 good hard smacks across her bottom . . . the youngest got 18 with it yesterday for leaving her room untidy and insolence . . . I would certainly recommend it for teenage girls, and would not hesitate to use it on the bare bottom if, and when, deserved.'

Even when mothers do not directly beat their children, some appear to keep a close watch on the results in order to ensure that sufficient punishment has been meted out. After explaining that she usually beat her son and two daughters, another correspondent added that her husband would also give them a 'sound thrashing' when necessary. This took place 'upstairs in their bedroom with their pants or knickers down'. Afterwards 'I always inspect their bottoms to make sure they have had what they deserve.' She concludes with the hope that it will be possible to stop using the cane or the 'divided strap' on them once they are past their seventeenth birthday!

Commenting on the fact that such punishments are often associated with perverse enjoyment, the editor expresses amazement that anybody should regard beatings as sexually stimulating. '*Family View* recognises this, but frankly cannot quite comprehend it. To us a cane is for use as a mild punishment when all else has failed.'

A survey of their readers carried out by the same magazine provides interesting insights into the type of parents who still believe in physically punishing their children.

A majority (65 per cent) said that their politics were middle-of-the-road while the remainder claimed to be right-wing. They were mainly middle-class families in terms of income and most sent their children to state schools. Over half attended church regularly and most of those insisted that their children went as well. Some 70 per cent said that they were bringing up their children more strictly than their own upbringing.

In summary then, it appears that the initial bonding between human infants and their mothers is controlled by a powerful genetic programme.

Even with biological releasers on their side, however, many infants still suffer brutally at their parents' hands, or by their parents' commands, often in the name of love.

MOTHER LOVE AS EROTICISM
When discussing the bond between mother and child, most experts prefer to describe the relationship as one of 'attachment' rather than 'attraction' in order to distinguish it from the emotions present in a romantic attraction. Others, however, consider that the relationship is, in fact, a sexual or romantic one.

Some evidence for this may lie in the fact that a prohibition on incest can be found in virtually every form of human society, from the most modern to the most primitive. The powerful and universal nature of this taboo has encouraged some specialists to devote considerable time and effort to investigating the idea that when men marry they are really seeking mother substitutes.

Karl Jung believed that something very close to this accounted for the behaviour of some of his patients. According to his view, we carry deep within us a 'perfect mother' archetype – a primeval image of an all-powerful, nurturing and protective mother. Thus, men who seek out older women, or women with 'motherly' qualities do so because they were denied these qualities by their own mothers, and so spend their lives in an ultimately futile quest for the perfect mother in wife or lover.

Since no woman can ever meet the expectations produced by such an archetype, the search inevitably ends in frustration and disappointment that may be severe enough to produce a breakdown.

But while Jung's views were undoubtedly controversial, they provoked much less popular excitement and indignation than those of Freud who shocked respectable, middle-class Viennese society with his emphasis on infant sexuality and the proposal that the love of a male child for his mother was overtly sexual. Freud considered that the unresolved conflict between a young male child's sexual feelings and his fear of retribution from a jealous father ranked as a primary cause of mental disorder.

He named this phenomenon the 'Oedipus complex' after the Oedipus, son of King Laius of Corinth. To avert a prophecy, Laius tried to kill his infant son by abandoning him on a mountainside. But the child was saved and raised by shepherds. As an adult he unknowingly slew his father and then, having been crowned King of Thebes, married Jocasta his mother without either knowing the incestuous nature of their relationship. When the terrible truth became known, Jocasta hanged herself while Oedipus tore out his own eyes.

In Freud's view this tragedy from the mythology of Greece was being played out in drawing-rooms and nurseries the length and breadth of Europe. Not in terms of physical murder, suicide and self-mutilation but at a deep, subconscious level where the powerful emotions aroused led to trauma and neuroses.

According to Freud, the child's sexual feelings develop during the first year of life and culminate, around the age of seven, in the *phallic stage* during which desire is turned outwards and takes the form of being sexually attracted by the mother.

The guilt and fear aroused by these feelings are then repressed, and having been pushed deep into the subconscious remain a potent driving force which, without benefit of psychoanalysis, must forever remain below the level of awareness. These repressed feelings continue to inhibit the male throughout his life and shape his relationships with all other women.

Until recently it was assumed, as Freud later came to accept, that many of the stories of sexual abuse recounted by his patients were no more than fantasies. Modern surveys, however, suggest that, especially where girls are concerned, the incest taboo may be violated far more frequently than was previously recognised.

A three-year UK study, whose findings were published in 1984, concluded that one in ten British adults, amounting to more than four million, had been sexually abused before the age of sixteen and that the vast majority of these assaults were committed by parents. Most of the victims, however, were girls and 70 per cent of their abusers fathers or step-fathers, with the assaults mainly occurring between the age of six and ten. Sexual relations between mothers and their sons appear to be a far rarer form of abuse, although it undoubtedly does occur and was made the subject of a controversial French film.

MOTHER LOVE AS SELFLESS SACRIFICE

An Indian legend tells how a young man, driven half-crazy by his passion for a beautiful girl, demanded to know what he must do to win her love.

The girl, who was as wicked as she was lovely, hated the man's mother who had once insulted her. In revenge for this slight, she demanded that her lover slay his mother, then cut out the woman's heart and bring it to her as proof that the terrible crime had been committed.

Blind with desire, the youth murdered his mother and cut out her heart. Clutching the bloody relic to him, he hurried back to the girl. Missing his footing on the uneven ground, he fell heavily. At once the heart cried in anguish: 'My son, my poor son, have you hurt yourself?'

It is a story which embodies much of what many people hold to be true and precious about a mother's love for her children. A devotion blind to their faults and failings. A desire to care for and protect them from harm. A readiness to suffer any sacrifice, risk any danger, endure any hardship in their service.

So powerful are these ideas, and so fundamental are they considered to the role of mother, that they are frequently transferred to abstract or non-human entities which are then regarded as mother substitutes. These include the earth itself, nation states, and organised religions.

When Junius Brutus, a distinguished Roman patriot, was told by the Delphic oracle that the next consul would be he who first kissed his mother, the quick-thinking Brutus flung himself to the ground and cried out: 'Thus, then, I kiss thee Mother Earth.' The ploy succeeded and he was elected consul.

Countries generally become the motherland only at times of crisis or when their citizens are being exhorted to die in large numbers for no good reason.

At such times the concept of the Nation as mother is frequently elevated to elegiac heights. The first lines of Laurence Binyon's poem 'For The Fallen' provides a classic example: 'With proud thanksgiving, a mother for her children, England mourns for her dead across the sea.'

'Barbara Frietchie', a Civil War poem by John Greenleaf Whittier which many consider an outstanding achievement in popular American literature, symbolises the ideas of both motherhood and patriotic courage. As rebel troops under General Stonewall Jackson enter the town of Frederick, the redoubtable Barbara Fritchie, 'took up the flag the men hauled down'. Then holding it to her body she defies the army with the immortal cry: 'Shoot if you must this old gray head, but spare your country's flag, she said.'

So moved was the General by this appeal that he cautioned his troops: 'Who touches a hair of yon gray head, dies like a dog! March on! he said.'

Here the mythical Barbara Fritchie is seen as employing the qualities of motherhood in a patriotic cause, while the general, responding with filial respect, extends her his protection.

This vision of motherhood as sacrifice, the willing sacrificial lamb giving up life, liberty and the pursuit of happiness for the sake of her children, exerts a social influence which should not be under-estimated. It is, I believe, the basis of many of our most deeply held, yet least often articulated, beliefs about the role of mothers in the family and, by extension, of the women's role in society.

MOTHER LOVE AS MYSTICISM
In religion the term 'mother goddess' has been applied to deities who personify the female principles of life giving and fertility. Among Babylonians and Assyrians her common name was Ishtar, and she was the goddess of both love and war, identified in astrology with the planet Venus. Revered as the source and protector of life and fruitfulness, it was through her bounty that nature revived each springtime, while the decay of autumn and the gloom of winter symbolised the withdrawal of her care. According to mythology she descends to the lower world as summer ends and remains a prisoner until spring. Rites in celebration of Ishtar included love-making, and later these became the excuse for orgies on a grand scale and sacred prostitution in the temples where she was worshipped.

In various guises Ishtar dominated religious belief throughout Asia Minor for centuries. In Phrygia, the most celebrated mother-goddess was Cybele, frequently termed 'Great Mother', *in whose honour castrated priests performed sacred rituals*.

A feature of all such goddesses was the idea of procreation, the creation of life either through their own, unaided efforts – for this reason they were sometimes termed 'virgin mothers' – or with the help of a youthful male companion. On occasions her young consort was thought to be her son, although he was also seen as the object of her desires. His death brings about the sorrows of autumn and winter. His resurrection signals the start of spring.

In Egyptian mythology, the mother-goddess was Isis, whose

special function was held to be fertility and the securing of a natural bond of affection between parents and their children. It seems likely that these beliefs originated in early societies where men were nomadic hunters and herdsmen, while the women remained with their kinsfolk and, by maintaining a more or less permanent residence, formed the stable unit of society. Because each woman had several husbands (polyandry), the line of descent was passed down through the female blood-line, and it was therefore the woman who became associated with the life-sustaining forces.

As society became increasingly male-dominated, old goddesses were replaced by masculine deities although mother-goddesses continued to flourish in the eastern Mediterranean long after they had disappeared from other parts of Asia. She took her place alongside the divine father and her youthful companion, whose role had previously been vague, was firmly established as her son.

In other cultures, however, the female goddess remained supreme, for example in Indian religions, and may also account for the veneration of the Virgin Mary in Christianity. Indeed it may well have been the traditional desire of Mediterranean peoples for a mother-goddess that influenced the early Christian church to perceive Mary as a divine virgin mother whose divine son was begotten by a supreme father-god. Belief in the virgin birth was widespread by the second century AD and became part of the earliest creeds.

It was not until later, however, that Mary was regarded as having remained a virgin even after the birth of Christ and having herself been conceived 'without sin'.

MOTHER LOVE AS SMOTHER LOVE
Although a mother's love for her children is generally held to be among the purest and most selfless of all human emotions, many also recognise its Jekyll and Hyde quality. There is a capacity in this love, when it becomes too intense and relentless, to transform sacrifice into suffocating selfishness, creating a psychological straitjacket that warps the emotional growth of both mother and child.

A chilling example of the almost pathological mutual dependence which may then develop is provided by psychiatrist Dr Oliver Sacks in his remarkable book *Awakenings*.

As a psychiatrist in New York's Mount Carmel Hospital, Dr Sacks found he had under his care several victims of a strange and terrible epidemic which swept the world at the end of the First World War. Called 'the Sleeping Sickness' (Encephalitis Lethargica) it produced a form of Parkinson's disease which left the victims severely mentally and physically disabled. Hundreds of thousands were affected before the epidemic burned itself out and vanished as mysteriously as it had arisen. Unable to care for themselves, subjected to violent muscular spasms or trapped between life and death in a strange and terrible catatonic state, the sufferers had to rely on the care of relatives or end their days in places like Mount Carmel.

One such patient was Lucy K., a woman whose appearance Dr Sacks describes as being both pathetic and grotesque. A heavy and powerfully built woman who looked much younger than her age – a common feature of the disease – she was waited on every day by her mother. While this woman's devotion was undoubted, the price for her attention and self-sacrifice was a high one. In return for attention and care, she demanded that her adult daughter stay for ever in a state of childlike dependence. Like Peter Pan, Lucy K. was never allowed to grow up. Each day her mother would comb and groom her daughter's hair, then carefully make-up her face so that, with her jet-black hair heavily braided and her unlined face painstakingly powdered, she was transformed into a grotesque parody of a human being, part infant and part adult. For Oliver Sacks 'She looked like – I could never decide: like a clown, or a geisha, or Miss Haversham, or a robot. But most of all like a baby-doll, in the most absolute and literal sense of the words: a living reflection of her mother's mad whim.'

The doctor quickly saw that his patient's mental and physical state could not be viewed in isolation since both were inexorably bound up with her mother's feelings and behaviour. Her inability to speak, for example, perfectly reflected the woman's paranoid warnings never to talk to anybody else since the whole world was her enemy. Only her mother could be trusted, talked to, confided in. Only her mother was an ally in a world otherwise uniformly hostile and unwaveringly hazardous.

Dire warnings were alternated with hours of crooning, maudlin baby-talk: 'Lucy, my baby, my little living doll . . . There's nobody who loves you like me . . . Nobody in the world *could* love you like me . . . For you, little Lucy, I have given my life . . .'

Although Lucy's mother arrived at the hospital early and never left until late, and although she was quite truthful in her avowal that she had sacrificed twenty-five years of her life to her daughter's care, Dr Sacks had no difficulty in recognising the contradictory nature of her attitude which 'involved hatred, sadism, and destructiveness no less than inordinate love and devotion.'

While this is clearly an extreme example of mutual dependence and an adult's refusal to permit an escape from childhood, similar patterns of dominance and dependency can be found in many normal families.

'All women become like their mothers. That is their tragedy,' wrote Oscar Wilde in *The Importance of Being Earnest*. 'No man does. That's his.' It's a familiar quotation which captures something of the essence of the relationship between mothers and their children that is, so often, part-reflection and part-rejection. On occasions a mirroring of the mother's attitudes and feelings and at other times a search for independence from such emotional moulding: it is an ambivalence which, as Wilde implies, exists not only in the relationship between mothers and children, but in the attitudes towards women many males come to hold.

MOTHER LOVE AS A SOURCE OF MALE AMBIVALENCE

The stand-up comic's wife and mother-in-law jokes, sexual discrimination at work and the exploitation of women in strip clubs, massage parlours and hardcore pornography share a common theme with St Paul's caution to the Corinthians that: 'It is better to marry than to burn'.

An essentially fearful and ambivalent attitude of men towards women exists and its origins can be traced to the cradle. Women are essential for the continuation of the species, yet marriage is little more than a distasteful necessity to be avoided whenever possible, and abandoned at the earliest convenient moment. Women are seen as being at the same time both predatory and protective, sexually promiscuous yet parsimonious in their favours which must be won from them by bribery, or taken from them by force; capricious and constant; desirable but dangerous; subservient yet unreliable.

Dorothy Dinnerstein, Professor of Psychology at Rutgers University, attributes these feelings, in part, to the fact that 'the early mother, monolithic representative of nature, is a source like nature of ultimate distress as well as ultimate joy. Like nature she is both nourishing and disappointing, both alluring and threatening, both comforting and unreliable.'

The infant, she says, loves his/her mother's shape, taste, warmth, sound and movement in the same way that she, or he, is delighted by the charms of nature, the dancing of sunlight, the warmth of a quilt, animals and birds. Yet this love is mixed with hatred because, like nature, the mother fails to provide full protection and provision for her/his bodily needs. All babies, no matter how well looked after, are hungry at times, cold on occasions, frightened by sudden sights and sounds, by mysterious movements or unexpected disturbances.

'The mother, then – like nature, which sends blizzards and locusts as well as sunshine and strawberries – is perceived as capricious and sometimes actively malevolent,' writes Dorothy Dinnerstein in *The Rocking of the Cradle*. 'Her body is the first important piece of the physical world that we encounter, and the events for which she seems responsible the first instances of fate. Hence Mother Nature, with her hurricane daughters Alice, Betty, Clara, Debbie, Edna. Hence that fickle female, Lady Luck.'

It may appear that in exploring these poetic, social and religious aspects of motherhood we have moved away from modern thoughts and feelings about mother love. However, it is only by appreciating the many strands of thought, feeling, belief and attitudes that one can begin to understand the enormously complex and powerful emotions involved in mother love. A relationship based on biological mechanisms, shaped by ancient traditions, and coloured by our cultural heritage.

Of course mothers love their children for reasons which have nothing to do with biological bonding or cultural conditioning. Yet we cannot ignore any of these influences when considering the potency of the five myths of mother love described at the start of this chapter. For their influence over the lives of each of us is considerable.

The myth that natural mothers are always the best people to raise their own children, for example, means that well-meaning courts and social workers not infrequently remove previously neglected or battered children from loving foster homes and return them to their mothers, sometimes with disastrous consequences.

Yet research has shown that a mother's love, while desirable, is clearly not essential to a child's successful development. Indeed the views put forward by psychologist John Bowlby in his influential report to the World Health Authority, in 1951, that it is 'essential for mental health . . . that the infant and young child should experience a warm, intimate and continuous relationship with his mother . . .' are now regarded as incorrect. 'Monotropy', as the need for an attachment to just one person is called, has been effectively refuted by more recent research. Rudolph Schaffer and Peggy Emerson, for instance, have shown that by the end of the first year, the time when babies first start showing attachment to particular people, 29 per cent showed an attachment to more than one person, and 10 per cent to five or more. Six months later, 87 per cent were attached to more than one person and around a third showed attachment to five or more. American studies have also shown that young children can become as attached to their father as to their mother. A study by Thomas Weisner and Ronald Gallimore of 186 non-industrial societies, where it is more common for a large number of people to care for the child, revealed that in only five of them was the mother rated as the 'almost exclusive' caretaker.

'This seems sufficient evidence to discredit the idea that a continuous relationship with *one* caretaker, the mother or "mother-substitute" is essential,' says Dr Peter Smith, who suggests that children can probably cope with receiving care from up to 30 different people, although he cautions that the child's age and personality are important factors in the equation.

What seems clear, however, is that the notion that 'mother knows' best and a 'woman's place is in the home' owes more to tradition than either biological necessity or psychological need.

Equally adults who feel they do not love their mother sufficiently, or indeed at all, may have grounds for regret but none for self-recrimination. Just as there are no natural laws which inevitably cause mothers to love their children, neither is it carved in stone that children who fail to love their mothers are abnormal.

It is, in fact, a belief which actually inhibits the growth of a healthy relationship between mother and child by imposing limitations on sharing of ideas, opinions and experiences. The desire to keep certain things from their mother because she would be hurt, or angry, or disappointed – in other words that the extent of their love might be called into question – exerts a powerful censorship over what can or cannot be admitted in many households.

Many gay men and women, for example, state that the hardest thing they ever have to do is admit their sexual preferences to their parents and especially to their mother. Even those who have come to terms with their orientation and feel neither guilt nor anxiety about it will shrink from discussions with the parents and, often, especially with their mother.

When a French sociologist, Elizabeth Badinter, challenged the whole concept of a mothering instinct in her 1980 book *L'Amour en plus* it created an uproar among the nation's 20 million women.

According to one reviewer it produced: 'An electric shock among the French public which, in a period of changing values, is hanging on to the idea of universal mother love as a last refuge.'

That refuge, although based on biology and fabricated from centuries of tradition, seems about to be laid waste. While some may find this threatening, others will surely see it as the dawning of a healthier and more mature day. A too long delayed reassessment of this most basic, complex and profoundly influential of all human attraction is much needed. It is the only attraction, which, for better or worse, shapes the future of us all.

8

Loathe at first sight?

You've got to be taught to hate and fear,
You've got to be taught from year to year.
It's got to be drummed in your dear little ear,
You've got to be carefully taught

Oscar Hammerstein II
South Pacific

The vote was more than unanimous – many of the mob raised both hands – and the sentence was death. Osvaldo Pieres, 33, was given time to drain his glass of cheap white rum, and allowed to smoke a last cigarette. Then they dragged the self-confessed petty criminal from his stool in the seedy bar and clubbed the life out of him. The vigilantes were in no hurry. It took twenty minutes for Pieres to die.

The lynch-law execution of Osvaldo, in April 1983, was no isolated incident. In Brazil such rough justice has become not only more commonplace but increasingly socially acceptable. A newspaper poll found that almost half the local residents of the working class area of Saõ Paulo approved of public lynchings, a depth of feeling which produced 13 vigilante killings in just four months and involved some 500 normally law abiding citizens.

'The country has turned to taking justice into its own hands,' commented the district police chief Roberto Carvalho. In part the almost open activities of lynch mobs can be explained by a sharp increase in crime coupled with accusations of ineffective – even non-existent – law enforcement. The same newspaper poll showed that 58 per cent of the working-class population had lost all confidence in the police.

But Brazilian social scientists suggested that the sudden fashion for mob violence also revealed deeper and more fundamental fears and frustrations.

'Lynching is a collective revolt,' says sociologist Maria Victoria Benevides, who pointed out that it was no coincidence it was confined to the poorest, most deprived, neighbourhoods which lacked not only effective policing, but almost every other civilised amenity: schools, paved roads, health care, electricity and sewers.

The idea that hatred and hostility towards individuals or minority groups is an expression of frustration, was first proposed more than forty years ago, by Professor John Dollard of Yale University. As we shall see there is considerable evidence, both experimental and anecdotal, to support this view. But before we look at the effects of frustration on people's attitudes, let's consider the various kinds of emotions that have to be explained.

First there is 'loathe at first sight!' Those occasions when we almost immediately take against the other person. There are, of course, times when this initial antagonism is justified by subsequent events. An unpopular officer in the TV series M.A.S.H. once asked one of his fellow doctors why everybody took such an instant dislike to him. 'Because it saves time, Frank,' came the laconic reply. But, on other occasions, we find that our original antipathy changes to one of liking, as we get to know them better, or at least grows into a grudging respect.

Secondly there is loathing which builds slowly, often arising from an original deep attraction. As the seventeenth-century playwright William Congreve astutely observed: 'Heav'n has no rage as love to hatred turned.'

Finally, we have prejudice against groups of people in which ill-feeling towards a particular individual is based solely on his, or her, membership of that group. They are hated, persecuted, discriminated against, purely as a consequence of their skin colour, religious or political beliefs, sexual orientation and so on.

The questions for which we must seek answers include: Are such aggressive responses born into us or, as Oscar Hammerstein suggested, taught us?

If learned, to what extent can prejudice be deliberately manipulated for reasons of personal hatred or political advantage? Equally, to what extent can prejudice, racial hatred, religious intolerance, bigotry and discrimination be eliminated by education, legal intervention, social work programmes and counter-propaganda?

In his satirical lyric *National Brotherhood Week*, Tom Lehrer takes a fairly pessimistic view of officially inspired attempts at reconciliation. After all, he points out, black hates white, rich hate poor, Protestants hate Catholics, Catholics hate Protestants, Moslems hate Hindus, and all of his folk hate all of your folk, a fact he ironically described as 'American as apple pie!'

When trying to disentangle the various threads of feeling which go to make up the usually complex emotions of counter-attraction, simply asking people why they feel as they do is seldom much help. For one thing we rarely really know what makes us dislike one person, despise another, and loathe a third.

Often, all one can do is echo the words of Thomas Brown, which were quoted at the start of this book,

> I do not like thee, Doctor Fell,
> The reason why I cannot tell;
> But this I know, I know full well,
> I do not like thee Dr Fell.

When explanations are offered they are often irrational and may not present an honest picture of that person's feelings. You may be told, for instance that: 'He's got a weak chin'; 'She's too intellectual'; 'He doesn't take life seriously enough'; 'She's too ambitious.'

Justifications are especially unreliable when the real source of dislike is religious, racial, political, or sexual, rather than openly expressed sentiments which would brand people as intolerant or prejudiced. For instance, one investigator was told: 'I've nothing against homosexuals, but what I really dislike is the way they've perverted that attractive English word "Gay".'

While attempts by psychologists to explore negative feelings in a more rational and scientific manner have not provided complete answers to the questions raised above, they have allowed us important insights into the nature of dislike, and the ways by which people can deliberately mould emotions to suit their own purposes.

We'll start by looking at frustration and the role of scapegoats, who may be individuals or groups of people, in acting as a focus of those frustrations. These emotional responses tend to be among the most powerful and potentially destructive which can be unleashed in society. They are also amongst the easiest to manipulate, as both modern history and recent events have made all too terribly clear.

THE HUMAN SCAPEGOATS

In the 1930s, two American researchers, Carl Hovland and Robert Sears, made a remarkable discovery. By studying the price of cotton during the years 1882 and 1930, they found they were able accurately to predict the number of blacks lynched in the Deep South during any given year. The relationship was a simple one. The lower the market prices the more active the lynch mobs. In other words, economic depression led to suffering, frustration and the desire for scapegoats which in turn led to the brutal murders of innocent negroes.

Here, for probably the first time, a clear link had been established between frustration and the violent expression of latent racial prejudice. With tragic irony, even as Hovland and Sears were carrying out their research, the Nazis were preparing an even more horrifying demonstration of the ways in which minority groups – not only Jews but also gypsies, communists, homosexuals, and members of religions opposed to the Third Reich – could become the innocent victims of deliberately manipulated mass hatred.

It's not only society which demands scapegoats of course. Virtually every school, factory, and office in the world has at least one person who regularly gets blamed when things go wrong. On any playground there will be one child who get's picked on, in every army barracks one guy everybody else seems to hate, shun and regularly insult. In families too, especially in large families, it's not uncommon to discover an individual – not always a child – who is the focus for everybody else's resentments and misfortunes.

Where children are concerned the role of scapegoating can be forced on them quite early in life as I discovered when studying relationships in play-groups.

One particular boy was regarded as so disruptive that the adults took to saying 'Oh God, John . . .' whenever he came to the group. After a short while 'Oh God, John' was the almost automatic reaction whenever a child burst into tears, a toy was broken, a game degenerated into boisterous horse-play, a wall was scribbled on or paint spilled. Long after John has ceased to be troublesome he was still getting the blame if things went wrong.

THE LONG HISTORY OF SCAPEGOATS

Mosaic law among the Hebrews, included a special ceremony which took place in the temple on the Day of Atonement. In this ritual purification of collective sins, two goats were brought to the altar of the tabernacle where the high priest cast lots for them, one for the Lord, the other for Azazel, the rebel angel whom God is said to have cast out of Heaven for refusing to worship Adam.

The Lord's goat was then sacrificed, while the other had the citizens' dark deeds, their evil thoughts and guilty actions, transferred to it through acts of confession. Its life spared, the scapegoat was then driven out of the city gates and allowed to escape into the wilderness, carrying away all wickedness with it.

But the idea of using scapegoats as a means of absolving individuals or whole communities from sin, was not confined to the Hebrew faith. A belief that evil and sin are a form of dangerous contagion, either caught from a bad person or the result of witchcraft, is common to many religions. Wickedness is purged by transferring its infection to another human being, an animal, plant or some ritual object. This is then either destroyed or, as in the case of the Hebrew scapegoat, driven out of the community.

Animals were used by the ancient Chinese and Babylonians. Among the Pacific Islanders evil is transferred to a plant which is then thrown into running water. The impurities of the Japanese people are ritually purged, twice yearly, during the ceremony of O'Hari. Conducted by the Emperor or his representative, this involves transferring the taint of impurity to objects which are then either washed or thrown into the water so that the contagion can be carried away. Each year the aborigines of Borneo launch a small boat laden with the sins and misfortunes of the nation which they believe will fall on the first vessel unfortunate enough to encounter it.

In early Roman and Greek civilisations communal sins were passed onto human victims who were then sacrificed, an idea implicit in the Christian belief that Christ died to purge the sins of humanity.

Scapegoating, therefore, has deep cultural roots, is very widely practised and inextricably linked to the concept of sacrifice. This, in turn, is an essential feature of most primitive religions and a prominent idea in many of the more advanced ones, including Christianity in some of its phases. The exact significance of the sacrifice is a matter of debate among theologians, and a number of explanations have been put forward of which two are of special interest here.

The widely held *substitutionary theory* claims that sacrifice provides an expiation for sin and that the death of the sacrificial animal serves as a substitution for the death of the sinful individual who makes the sacrifice. As you can see this is the essential nature and purpose of the scapegoat.

By contrast the *sacramental theory*, popular among anthropologists, takes the idea a step further by interpreting the sacrifice as an intermediary between the sacred and the profane. Here it becomes the means by which a sinful person frees himself, or herself, from the restrictions, limitations and taboos – supernatural prohibitions – created by profanity, and is able to enjoy elevation to the status and privileges of the sanctified. In other words it has a positive, rather than merely a negative virtue. By using a scapegoat sins are not only painlessly purged but the individual making that sacrifice is able to gain in spiritual stature.

This strongly suggests that by directing hatred towards a person or group of people, the prejudiced are not simply venting frustrations, they are cleansing themselves of their own sins – including presumably the sin of prejudice and hatred – and so gaining a sense of righteous promotion. These feelings of redemption and purification may account for the often reported fact that crimes of barbaric cruelty can be performed by perfectly ordinary, peace-loving and 'godly' men and women.

After Osvaldo Pires had been clubbed slowly to death, the neighbourhood rapidly returned to normal. Men who had, only moments before, been lashing his broken body with bloody staves, returned to their drinks at the bar as if nothing had happened. While his body was still in the street, women who had witnessed the execution went on with their shopping, children played unconcernedly.

SCAPEGOATING AND SELF-SACRIFICE
Extending this notion, it becomes easier to understand what a powerful influence the idea of self-sacrifice can exert when it comes to persuading the citizens of one country to wage war on those of another. In his 1914 poem *Peace*, Rupert Brooke exactly captures this delight in the possibility of self-sacrifice as a process of purification.

Now, God be thanked Who has matched us with His hour,
  and caught our youth, and wakened us from sleeping.

He then presents an analogy between spiritual cleansing through sacrifice in battle and physical cleansing in water 'as swimmers into cleanness leaping' in order to free oneself of the wickedness of a world 'old and cold and weary' where honour and morality have long since perished.

I raise this now because, as the chapter will show later, the role of the aggressor and the attitude of the selected scapegoat are not independent but intricately intertwined. It is wrong, for instance, to assume that victims of such attacks are always helpless and reluctant. They frequently are, of course, and I am certainly not saying that the persecuted invariably carry a measure of blame for their sufferings. But it is equally true that their reaction to aggression, individually and collectively, must always exert some degree of influence over the course and intensity of their persecution.

'The general picture of scapegoating that emerges is that individuals tend to displace aggression onto groups that are visible, that are relatively powerless, and that are disliked to begin with,' says Elliot Aronson, Professor of Psychology at the University of California, in his book *The Social Animal*. He makes the important point that the form which this aggression takes will depend on what is allowed or approved by the group committing the aggression. It will also depend on the response of the victims themselves.

The British psychologist Anthony Storr sees weakness as an important factor in increasing the hostility and violence of an aggressor. In *Human Aggression* he notes that: 'In human beings, a show of weakness on the part of the defeated is as likely to increase hatred as to restrain it.' This response is a rather curious one biologically, since the appeasement signals by defeated animals usually reduce or bring to an end the attack on them; amongst humans, however, appeasement often has entirely the opposite effect.

Drawing together the ideas already discussed, a possible explanation for this paradoxical behaviour emerges. For a sacrifice to be effective the scapegoat must be 'worthy'. Animals slain at pagan altars were never weaklings, the runt of the litters, so unhealthy they had little or no commercial value. On the contrary, those sacrificed were usually the most beautiful, costly and valued beasts. Similarly human sacrifices were selected from among the youngest, strongest, and most handsome of the race. Anything less than perfection was almost certain to be treated by the gods with contempt and the sacrifice rejected.

Since self-abasement, appeasement and the rejection of force as a means of settling arguments are generally interpreted as signs of weakness or cowardice in Western culture, it follows that the 'sacrifice' of such people is held to be less worthy. In order to enhance their feelings of self-righteousness and intensify the cathartic purification obtained, aggressors resort to compensatingly greater aggression.

The idea that the victim must be 'worthy' of the fate intended for him is a common one in European literature especially where the theme is one of patriotic self-sacrifice. Writing in 1906, Rudyard Kipling perfectly caught the mood that would prevail at the outbreak of war eight years later when he wrote in *The Children's Song* from *Puck of Pooks Hill*:

Teach us to rule ourselves alway,
Controlled and cleanly night and day;
That we may bring, if need arise,
No maimed or worthless sacrifice.

The idea that the victim actually plays some role in his, or her, eventual fate is a fairly recent, and more than a little controversial notion. But where scapegoats are concerned there is good evidence to show that the relationship between attacker and attacked is far more complex than generally supposed.

THE CREATION OF SCAPEGOATS

The fact that the Nazis' persecution of the Jews made no distinction between social class, wealth or status, strongly suggests that despite Hitler's early attempts to justify his anti-semitism in political and economic terms their motivations were mainly psychological.

Scientific evidence for this suggestion can be found in an experiment carried out in the late Forties by two American psychologists, Neal Miller of Rockefeller University and Richard Bugelski of SUNY College, Buffalo, who recruited 31 volunteers from among young men attending a summer camp.

The investigators first asked them to take a series of long, boring and mentally demanding exams which, they were falsely told, formed part of the educational programme. In order to produce the maximum amount of frustration the tests were made so difficult that everybody was bound to fail miserably.

Then, to rub salt into the wound, the testing sessions were deliberately allowed to run overtime so that the hapless volunteers found themselves missing the only entertainment on offer all week, a popular film in the camp cinema. Before subjecting them to this ordeal the psychologists had assessed the men's attitudes toward Mexicans and Japanese. After they had completed the exams these attitudes were reassessed. In line with expectations the frustrated subjects showed an increase in prejudice while a control group, who had not been frustrated, did not alter their views.

A decade later, in a study along similar lines, Donald Weatherley, looked specifically at anti-Semitism by selecting a group of college students some of whom had expressed prejudice against Jewish people. They were shown pictures of men and women, some of whom had been given Jewish names, and asked to write stories about them. As in the Miller, Bugelski experiment some of the subjects were deliberately frustrated, while others were not. From this study two major findings emerged. The first was that people who are already anti-Semitic direct more aggression towards Jewish characters after being frustrated than those without such prejudice.

Secondly, Donald Weatherley was unable to find any differences between the two groups when the characters in the pictures did not have Jewish names.

In other words frustration tends to produce aggression directed specifically against somebody you already hate. But what creates this hatred to begin with?

Ten years before Miller and Bugelski carried out their investigations, psychologist John Dollard was busy collecting data for what was to become a classic study of prejudice in smalltown USA.

He selected an industrial town, its main factories were sawmills, which had a significant minority of recently arrived German immigrants. At first these newcomers had lived harmoniously with their neighbours, then came the Wall Street crash and the Depression. As jobs became scarce, prejudice against Germans increased sharply. 'Local whites largely from the surrounding farms manifested considerable direct aggression towards the newcomers,' Dollard wrote. 'Scornful and derogatory opinions were expressed . . . and the native whites had a satisfying sense of superiority towards them.'

It was clear to him that the chief factor behind the rising hostility was competition for work and job status in the local timber factories: 'The native whites felt definitely crowded for their jobs by the entering German groups and in case of bad times had a chance to blame the Germans who by their presence provided more competitors for scarcer jobs. There seemed to be no traditional pattern of prejudice against Germans.'

A similar change of attitudes and increasing hostility against a minority group had been observed towards Chinese immigrant labour during the mid-nineteenth century. These men had been brought into the United States to build the transcontinental railways at a time when work was plentiful and their cheap labour in great demand.

Once the network was completed, however, prejudice quickly built up against these now non-essential newcomers. From being regarded as law-abiding, sober, hard-working and decent men and women they were soon being widely viewed as a dishonest, drunken, indolent and evil race responsible for most of society's ills. This hostility intensified with the ending of the Civil War, when returning soldiers put even greater pressure on the market for jobs in a Nation economically ravaged by years of fighting.

These findings highlight two important aspects of prejudice.

The first is that, as with any sort of attitude, there are three interlinked responses. Both the Germans, in Dollard's study, and the Chinese were thought of as wicked (an intellectual or cognitive element), they aroused powerful, negative, emotions among many whites (an affective component), and they were the victims of verbal abuse, physical assault and attacks on their property (the cognative component). Although the last need not always be present in prejudice – people may keep their feelings to themselves to avoid being unpopular or from fear of the law, the first two components are always found. They are the fertile soil from which aggression will arise given the right psychological and social climate.

Before widespread and overt attacks could be launched against the Jewish people, Nazi propaganda first embarked on a massive campaign of vilification during which they were accused of responsibility for every misfortune the Germans had suffered since 1918.

Defeat during the First World War, Hitler argued, occurred solely because the army at the front was betrayed on the homefront. A betrayal which, he claimed, had been led and supported by a Jewish conspiracy. Similarly, the harsh reparations forced on the German people by the Treaty of Versailles, had been planned and directed by Jews. Having accused them of responsibility for past miseries and humiliations, Hitler then charged them with even greater crimes in prospect. Were Germany to fall beneath their yoke, he claimed, it would not be long before the rest of the world followed. These outrageous claims had been made, and largely ignored outside the fledgling National Socialist Party, as early as 1924.

In *Mein Kampf* he asserted: 'If the Jew is victorious over the other peoples of the world, his crown will be the funeral wreath of humanity.' Finally, he absolved himself and his followers from any feelings of guilt over actions against the Jewish people by assuring them that anti-semitism was divinely inspired: 'I believe that I am acting in accordance with the will of the Almighty Creator,' Hitler told readers of *Mein Kampf*, 'By defending myself against the Jew, I am fighting for the work of the Lord.'

Here, then, are the three basic elements from which scapegoats can be created. Blame for everything which has gone wrong in the past. Accusations that even more horrendous crimes are being planned. Claims that your actions are either divinely inspired and/or justified by the demands of a higher authority; National security; Chairman Mao's Little Red Book; Lenin's speeches; the honour of the armed services.

But when choosing the individual, or individuals, who are to play the role of scapegoat it's useful to bear in mind an important additional qualification – the ease with which they can be dehumanised through the creation of stereotypes.

PROPAGANDA — THE BIRTH OF A STEREOTYPE

Just as any cartoonist or stage impersonator is immensely grateful when their intended victims have some feature by which the public will instantly recognise them, so the prejudiced and the propagandist alike search for some obvious characteristics in the minority group under attack. An aspect of face or body, skin pigmentation or hair colouring, style of dress or posture that offer raw materials for a thumb-nail sketch, a short-hand Identikit image, an immediately recognisable caricature.

When your victim's skin is black, brown or yellow, their features distinctive or the way they dress unusual the task is not difficult. If they look very much like the majority of the population it may be necessary to discover, or invent, a feature common to a few and apply it indiscriminately to them all. By this process Jews must always have large, hooked noses; Asians be slant-eyed; gay men be limp-wristed and gay women wear jack boots; while the Irish are seen as oafish bog-dwellers. It is no coincidence that since 1969, when civil war returned to Ireland, there has been a torrent of anti-Irish jokes whose purpose is to reinforce a stereotypic view of all Irish people as stupid, venal, uneducated and unreliable.

The purpose of the stereotype, then, is first to prevent people viewing the scapegoat group as human beings and secondly to offer a process by which this 'enemy' may be rapidly identified. Perhaps one of the reasons why the fifth columnist, like the double-agent or traitor, arouses such bitter hostility is that he, or she, had, until their betrayal was discovered, appeared just like 'one of us', a fully paid-up member in good standing of the silent majority.

The creation of stereotypes is greatly assisted by an important, yet little recognised, fact of human perception. Our view of the world is always highly subjective and highly selective. We do not scan our surroundings paying equal attention to each and every item of possible interest. Instead we narrow our focus to those things which seem of greatest importance or concern. This accounts for the familiar experience of buying a make of car you regard as fairly unusual and suddenly finding that everybody else seems to be driving the same model. Equally, it is a common experience among pregnant women that the streets overnight appear to be peopled by other women in an advanced state of pregnancy.

The prejudiced pay greater attention to anything that appears to reinforce their prejudices than to anything which challenges or might contradict these attitudes. In *Mein Kampf* Hitler provides an excellent illustration of this process in action: 'Since I had begun to concern myself with this question and to take cognisance of the Jews, Vienna appeared to me in a different light than before.

Wherever I went, I began to see Jews, and the more I saw, the more sharply they became distinguished in my eyes from the rest of humanity.'

When the persecution is State-inspired and directed you can enhance this process of selective attention by direct manipulation of the media. This can be done through careful sifting of events, as occurs in democracies, by direct censorship, as in Soviet Bloc countries, or through outright fabrication – what Western Intelligence agencies call 'disinformation'. But if you really want your propaganda to have an impact it needs to be presented in such a way as to ensure maximum emotional arousal.

Der Stürmer – a case in point

Although, as the National Socialists gained control over the media, the whole publishing, broadcasting and film industry was used to spread anti-Jewish propaganda, two journals specialised in virulent and undisguised anti-semitism from the start. One was *Der Stürmer*, the other, which never achieved Stürmer's notoriety, *Judenkenner*. Both were published by Julius Streicher who remained, until the end of the war, an honoured member of the Nazi party.

In *The House that Hitler Built*, historian Stephen Roberts describes how Streicher realised 'that a mixture of pornography and low racial diatribe could be made to pay, and Nazi organisations saw to it that his paper reached all party bodies and even the schools.'

Young people were actively encouraged to read *Der Stürmer* and absorb its nauseating falsehoods. Stephen Roberts remarks that one of the saddest sights he saw during his time in Germany was a group of fresh-faced teenagers at a Hitler Youth camp. After finishing a breath-taking gymnastics display, the youths gathered eagerly around a stall selling Streicher's paper and avidly studied its grotesque cartoons.

When Roberts asked his SS officer guide whether he did not see anything funny in *Der Stürmer*'s outrageous lies, the man replied bluntly: 'It is not funny. They must be taught the truth about the Jews. It is part of their spiritual upbringing.'

Later during his visit he heard an English peer speaking enthusiastically about the camp and comparing it to the Boy Scouts. 'Do you think you would let my son come here for a few months to get the spirit of it?' he inquired. As the aristocrat spoke, Roberts recalls looking at the growing groups around the newspapers and then at a cartoon in *Der Stürmer* which showed a Jew disembowelling a beautiful young German girl.

It was not by chance that Streicher peddled his anti-Semitic diatribes laced with 'jokes' and spiced with sex and violence. By arousing readers in this way its message of hatred was far more likely to make a powerful impact and to deepen feelings of hostility and revulsion towards the Jewish people. How and why this happens I will explain later in this chapter.

From the discussion so far, it seems clear that for prejudice to take hold and serve as the driving-force of a powerful counter-attraction, four conditions are necessary.

First there must be a sense of frustration, feelings of resentment and bitterness which may be quite general and free-floating, being directed towards the world at large rather than any particular group of individuals.

Secondly, there should be a belief that some minority is either in direct competition for scarce resources, jobs, status, housing etc. and/or that it appears in some reasonably plausible way to be responsible for the circumstances that created the feelings of frustration in the first place. During major strikes, workers going through the picket-lines immediately remove themselves from the striking majority and create a minority group simply by reason of their going on working. Thus the first two conditions are satisfied.

Thirdly, victims must be dehumanised by having their individuality replaced with a stereotype. One of the first stages is to call them by some derogatory name, 'Coon'; 'Yid'; 'Spick'; 'Mick'; 'Spade'; 'Poof'; 'Hun'; 'Commie'; 'Nip'; 'Gook' and so on.

In cases where prejudice is sanctioned by the State, numbers may be used in place of names, as in prisons, concentration camps and so on. Numbers in place of names are, of course, also used in order to create a feeling of intense involvement with a particular group, a point we shall discuss in a moment.

Finally, prejudice must be regarded as acceptable, if not to the great majority then at least to a significant minority among whom the prejudiced person can find support and encouragement for their views.

TOKENISM – HOW REVERSED PREJUDICE WORKS

'I'm certainly not prejudiced against blacks,' somebody protests, 'Why, I always give generously to African famine relief.'

This kind of concealed prejudice, is called tokenism. It may be linked to reverse discrimination, or 'a leaning over backwards' desire to treat minorities 'fairly'. Although this approach may sound less harmful than direct prejudice, it is, in fact, an extremely destructive attitude. For one thing it patronises the minority concerned, for another it is far harder to fight, and the attitudes behind it are often much more resistant to change, than blatant and unconcealed hostility.

Tokenism means being tolerant, or generous, over unimportant, trivial things while strongly resisting real change. You find this in remarks like: 'I don't mind sharing a table in a restaurant with one, but I'd never let him marry my daughter.'

In an experiment designed to study racial tokenism, white university students – who claimed to feel little or no racial prejudice – saw a series of slides showing interracial couples and black and white children playing together.

As they watched, they were falsely informed that equipment monitoring bodily responses was indicating a deep rooted hostility towards blacks. Following the slide show, subjects were sent to another part of the building where they were to be paid for taking part in the study. On their way, some were approached by a black man, others by a white man while a third group were allowed to make the trip unchallenged. In each case the men, confederates of the experimenter, begged for money.

The researchers predicted that subjects would respond more generously to the black beggar than to the white in order to bolster their unprejudiced self-image. This was, indeed, what happened with the black 'beggar' receiving more money than the white man.

The crucial part of this experiment came two days later when the subjects were asked for help by a fictitious organisation which claimed to be promoting racial tolerance on campus. They were asked to fill in a form committing themselves to various activities which ranged from the trivial – putting up posters for instance – to the time-consuming, such as agreeing to work in an information booth for ten hours a week. Here the prediction was that those who had given generously to the black man would be less likely to contribute time and effort to the cause than either students who had been importuned by the white man or not approached at all. In other words those who had handed out a few cents to the black would resort to 'tokenism' in order to sustain their 'non-prejudiced' self-image. Once again these predictions were strongly confirmed.

This experiment lends support to the feelings of many minority groups that the outright prejudices of the self-admitted bigot are actually easier to handle and less harmful in the long run than the tokenism of the pseudo-tolerant.

I have focused on prejudice at some length because it is such a widespread and enduring cause of hostility between individuals and between groups. When researchers studied the prejudices of Princeton undergraduates in 1933, they found strong agreement on the perceived characteristics of minority groups. As the table overleaf clearly shows, while the strength of stereotyped notions gradually declined during the following three decades, they by no means

134

disappeared, even in the supposedly laid-back and enlightened Age
of Aquarius.

Minority group	Characteristic	Percentage student agreeing		
		1933	1951	1967
Jews	shrewd	79	47	30
	mercenary	49	28	15
	ambitious	21	28	48
Blacks	superstitious	84	41	48
	lazy	75	31	26
	musical	26	33	47

(Adapted from Karlins, Coffman, and Walters 1969)

IN-GROUPS AND OUT-GROUPS
A feature common to many forms of prejudice and discrimination is
the idea of 'them and us', or as psychologists and sociologists prefer
to say 'in-groups' and 'out-groups'.

Let's start by making clear what we mean by 'groups' in order to
see how social scientists distinguish them from haphazard gather-
ings, such as shoppers in the same store or a theatre audience.

First of all, members of a genuine group have a sense of belonging
which comes from striving after a common goal. They share an
ideal, or an interest, they are gathered to solve a problem or fulfil a
purpose. This means, for example, that while ten strangers standing
around a bar and drinking would not comprise a 'group', in these
terms, ten drinkers who join Alcoholics Anonymous would con-
stitute a group since they share a common desire to break their
addiction.

Secondly, in a group, the fates of each individual member are
linked so that what happens to one of them in various ways affects
them all.

The term 'in-group' becomes appropriate the moment that a
group's structure is sufficiently established for it to have a clear and
clearly separate identity.

In war, informal groups often grow up because of the shared
dangers and experiences. A Second World War combat reporter,
Ernie Pyle, describes how in one camp the hundred men were like
members of a clan. 'They had all been together a long time and they
had almost a family pride in what they were doing and the machin-
ery they were doing it with.'

Commenting on the problems facing strangers drafted into such a tightly knit group, US war correspondent Bill Maudlin, explained that: 'Men in combat outfits kid each other around, they have a sort of family complex about it. No outsiders may join. . . . Bomber crews and paratroopers and infantry squads are about the same in that respect. If a stranger comes up to a group of them when they are bulling they ignore him. If he takes it upon himself to laugh at something funny they have said, they freeze their expressions, turn slowly around, stare at him until his stature has shrunk to about four inches and he slinks away . . .'

The shared cause that transforms individuals into a group range from fighting a war to running a charity, from membership of a secret society to following a particular football team. Yet despite these widely different purposes in-groups usually share basic features in addition to their members' sense of belonging and their interlinked destinies mentioned above.

There is often some form of initiation which would-be members need to satisfy before they are accepted, a process which typically involves an ordeal.

Ordeals may be haphazard and beyond the group's control, for example enduring the hardships and dangers of a front line unit or risking your life in a bomber. More often, however, they are formalised and remain more or less unchanged from one initiation ceremony to the next. Masonic Lodges, for instance, require new members to be initiated by means of a ceremony which includes, among other rituals, being blindfolded and baring the left breast.

Ordeals may be purely intellectual challenges, studying for a degree or writing a doctoral thesis in order to be accepted into the academic community; taking a Mensa IQ test; or sitting the Bar exams to qualify as a lawyer. But quite often they involve varying amounts of subordination, humiliation, isolation, deprivation and physical pain.

The life of a military cadet, described by Erving Goffman in his book, *Asylums*, offers a dramatic illustration of this process in action. As Goffman points out:

The recruit comes into the establishment with a certain conception of himself made possible by certain stable social arrangements in his home world. Upon entrance, he is immediately stripped of the support provided by these arrangements . . . he begins a series of abasements, degradations, humiliations, and profanations of self.

This clean break with the past must be achieved in a relatively short period. For two months, therefore, the swab is not allowed to leave the base or engage in social intercourse with non-cadets. This complete isolation helps to produce a unified group of swabs, rather than a heterogeneous collection of persons of high and low status . . . the role of the cadet must supersede other roles the individual has been accustomed to play.

But military establishments are far from unique in their use of pain and shame as part of their in-group initiation rights. In his history of the British public school, John Chandos explains that during the nineteenth century, such rites were widely practised. At Rugby and Harrow, initiation ceremonies included forcing boys to run the gauntlet while being beaten by their fellow pupils, or being 'stoned' with bread rolls baked as hard as pebbles.

At Winchester, which Chandos describes as 'at its *worst*, the most sinister of all schools' there was an institution called the 'tin gloves'. The junior's hand would be toughened by a burning brand of wood. Looking back over his schooldays in the 1840s, the Reverend William Tuckwell commented that, 'To this ordeal every junior was submitted . . . I was captured and my hand held fast and I can still recall the grinding thrill of pain as the glowing wood was pressed upon it by the ministering fiend.'

Finally it should be noted that rituals involving similar pain and humiliation are not confined to institutions. Many street gangs, for example, make similar demands on their members. In the Mafia, acceptance as a 'soldier' depends on committing some act of extreme violence, including murder. Gangs of football hooligans demand that each newcomer proves himself by some act of aggression against opposing fans.

In a study of football hooliganism, researchers from Leicester University recorded many conversations in which this sense of pride in 'doing well' by the gang was a recurring theme. After a foray into the opposing fans, one explained: 'When we come in like, down to the Leicester end they started singing "We're f- proud of you", you know and I felt f- brilliant after that, y'know when they was singin' that.'

EXPULSION FROM THE IN-GROUP

Degradation and humiliation are often part of a reverse initiation process as individuals are ceremonially expelled from in-group to out-group status.

Officers being dismissed from the service used to have their ranks of office ceremonially torn from their uniforms and their swords broken. In prisons the descent from free citizen to captive is also marked by a series of events calculated to break the will, dehumanise the victim – often in order to make it psychologically easier for guards to treat them – and emphasise their loss of rights, status, identity and individuality. Here's the way a female prisoner in Goffman's book describes the initiation of newcomers into the ways of prison life.

> First, there is the shower officer who forces them to undress, takes their own clothes away, sees to it that they take showers and get their prison clothes – one pair of black oxfords with cuban heels, two pairs of much-mended ankle socks, three cotton dresses, two cotton slips, two pairs of panties, and a couple of bras. Practically all the bras are flat and useless. No corsets or girdles are issued.
>
> There is not a sadder sight than some of the obese prisoners who, if nothing else, have been managing to keep themselves looking decent on the outside, confronted by the first sight of themselves in prison.

Violence too is often part of this transition. In *Surviving*, the Austrian psychologist Bruno Bettelheim describes how life in one of Hitler's concentration camps invariably began with extreme physical brutality. 'The transportation into the camp and the "initiation" into it was often the first torture which the prisoner had ever experienced and was, as a rule, physically and psychologically the worst torture to which the majority of prisoners were ever exposed. 'The initial torture, incidently, was called the prisoner's "welcome" to the camp by the gestapo.'

These tortures never lasted less than 12 hours and seldom more than 24. They included not only physical assaults, casual blows, and systematic beatings but verbal and psychological assaults. 'Prisoners', says Bettelheim, 'were forced to curse their God, make vile accusations against themselves and denounce their wives as prostitutes and adulteresses.' Its purpose was clear, he explains, to break the prisoner's will and to 'assure the guards that they really were superior to the prisoners'.

In *Borstal Boy*, Brendan Behan recounts his own painful introduction to penal life. After failing to call an officer 'Sir' he was struck savagely across the face.

> My head spun and burned and pained and I wondered would it happen again. I forgot and felt another smack, and forgot, and another, and moved, and was held by a steadying, almost kindly hand, and another, and my sight was a vision of red and white and pity-coloured flashes.

'You are looking at Mr Whitbread – what, Behan?'

I gulped and got together my voice and tried again till I got it out. 'I sir, please sir, I am looking at you, I mean, I am looking at Mr Whitbread, sir. . . .

Membership of an in-group need not imply hostility and antagonism towards out-groups, although there will always be attitudes of some kind between members of in-groups and those out-groups with whom they come into contact. The nature of these attitudes and whether they are warm and friendly or cold and hostile, depends on relationship between the two groups.

A prejudiced in-group, therefore, supports and encourages members in their view, views which might well be utterly repudiated by society as a whole. They offer a feeling of 'belonging', often to people who feel insecure and uncertain of themselves, and provide a justification for acts of violence, since each act then becomes a way of gaining more respect and attention from the other members.

TEACHING PEOPLE TO HATE

But there is another way too in which prejudiced in-groups build up their members' levels of intolerance and bigotry. This is through a process known technically as 'vicarious emotional conditioning'. It is a cumbersome phrase that describes a commonplace occurrence. People are affected by one another's emotions and when aroused by either strong positive or negative feelings we may attach these emotions to previously neutral people, objects or events.

Watch a cinema audience during a 'two handkerchief' weepy and many will be in tears; struck by terror during an especially frightening horror sequence, or sharing in the anger of an actor suffering 'injustice'. The more people there are to share an emotion the more powerful the effect of vicarious arousal. Even staunch internationalists, for instance, may find themselves moved to tears by the sound of their own National anthem being sung with fervour by a large crowd, while the same anthem sung just as sincerely by one or two people might produce nothing more than embarrassed irritation. It works with positive emotions too, of course, which is why comedy shows on TV use an audience or pretend they have by means of dubbed laughter.

In an experiment to investigate the power of this vicarious emotional arousal, Richard Lazarus showed adults a film of ritual circumcision among members of a primitive tribe. This portrayed, in full colour and great detail, the agony of a 14-year-old boy undergoing circumcision as part of his initiation into the tribe. As the child is held down by four men, the underside of his penis is seen being sliced open with a sharp piece of stone.

Richard Lazarus monitored the levels of physical arousal experienced by members of the audience during the showing of this film by means of electronic equipment. This revealed rapid increases in heart rate, blood pressure, respiration, sweating, and muscular tension at moments when the boy's expression gave the greatest indication of pain, but the levels dropped substantially during less traumatic scenes.

This may not sound especially surprising, since it fits in well with everyday experience and our own feelings about how we would be likely to respond under similar circumstances, but the implications of such results are considerable, since they give strong support to the view that emotions can be conditioned by observation as well as direct experience. Just watching somebody suffer pain, express anger or show signs of grief is sufficient to trigger the same feelings, often at a very high level, in ourselves. This reaction can then become the first stage in emotional conditioning.

To investigate the ways in which a neutral event can become a trigger for powerful emotions, through observation alone, S. M. Berger, asked people to watch a man, actually a stooge, being seemingly punished with powerful electric shocks. On every occasion when he was supposedly shocked the confederate would jerk up an arm as if in great pain.

While they watched, Berger's subjects were monitored for changes in their level of physical arousal. As in Lazarus's experiment, these increased every time the victim appeared to be in distress. Berger then sounded a buzzer a second or so before the 'shock' was administered and the man's arm jerked in 'anguish'.

After a time, the buzzer was sounded on occasions when the subject did not give any indication of pain. Despite this the subjects continued to show increases in physical arousal at every buzz. They had become conditioned to respond emotionally to the previously neutral sound of the buzzer.

To tie this finding into the creation of prejudice, imagine a child meeting members of some minority group. At first the other person is a neutral stimulus, just like Berger's buzzer, and does not produce any response. Now suppose that the child's parents, or members of an in-group, become emotionally aroused in the presence of that stranger. They show anger, or disgust, express hatred and rage. The more often these reactions are repeated the more likely it becomes that the once neutral stimulus will develop the power to trigger similar emotions.

Now think back to those boys in the Hitler Youth gathering

around Streicher's gutter-sheet, sniggering at the lewd cartoons and aroused by the sexual violence of the material. At the same time they are exposed to cartoon caricatures which emphasise certain physical features, associate Jewish men, women and children with every conceivable form of human wickedness and portray them as grotesques.

Here, then, is a perfect instrument for vicarious conditioning of their emotions.

Not only does it produce the necessary increases in physical and emotional arousal, which is immediately associated with a specific stimulus, but also provides the 'justifications' by which the children can 'explain' their feelings. 'I hate them because they are ugly . . .' 'I hate them because they are cruel . . .' 'I hate them because they are greedy . . .' and so on.

Finally, these attitudes are supported and encouraged by high status in-group members, parents and teachers, SS officers, government and so on.

Very similar techniques are widely used today, in books, newspapers and magazines, films, on television and in radio broadcasts. In some countries the propaganda is crude and, to sophisticated Western eyes, probably quite unbelievable. In Europe it tends to be more subtle, although the underlying mechanisms of arousal, association, and eventual conditioning through repetition remain. On occasions, however, the sledgehammer tactics of old-fashioned rabble-rousing are employed with apparent effect.

When *The Sun* newspaper, in Britain, announced the agonising death of more than 300 young Argentinians under the banner headline 'GOTTCHA!' many millions applauded. Yet only months earlier these same people, had they learned that the men had died as a result of drowning, burning, blasting and shredding with steel fragments in an industrial accident would probably have felt only horror and anger at the waste of healthy, young lives. Equally, news of the death of British sailors when *HMS Sheffield* was sent to the bottom, was the cause of rejoicing among Argentinians and was presented in a similarly simplistic and jingoistic manner by sections of their own press.

THE GROWTH OF HATRED

Even for a nation hardened to violence the message which came over Associated Press's wire from Houston was shocking. It described how three children, aged nine, eleven and twelve had beaten a four-year-old boy to death with savage blows to the head, chest and abdomen. The boy's five-year-old brother was also assaulted but survived. When asked why they had done it the children replied that it was for 'being bad' and said he had broken a model car.

Although children frequently squabble and fight, such excessive violence is, fortunately, extremely rare. Most of their battles are symbolic rather than serious, with youngsters shaping up to one another like two dogs preparing for a scrap that will be more found than fury, and more snarling than savagery.

This does not mean, of course, that children are without likes and dislikes, or that they are free from prejudices. These responses are not inborn, however, but grow slowly as a result of all that they see and hear around them. The views of the young child are, almost always, a reflection of parental opinions, attitudes and beliefs. While the majority of parents probably don't set out deliberately to create feelings of hostility towards certain groups of people, such lessons can be taught quite unintentionally through the process of vicarious emotional conditioning we discussed earlier. Because children admire their parents they imitate them as, later, they will imitate the views of other youngsters in their peer group. Prejudiced adolescents reveal their bigotry in rudeness and unqualified denunciations of those they regard as 'inferiors'. Their ill-manners not only give them satisfaction, but help reinforce these feelings of superiority.

They are suspicious of all who belong to the despised minority and feel certain of being tricked or cheated in any dealings with them. Probably the greatest psychological damage which the prejudiced adolescent suffers is that he, or (less often) she, achieves personal status in a quite unrealistic and unreasonable manner, through feelings of false superiority. In time this can lead to a maladjusted personality.

Prejudiced teenagers are often, themselves, victims of discrimination during childhood: 'A child who finds himself rejected and attacked on all sides is not likely to develop dignity and poise as his outstanding traits,' comments Harvard psychologist Professor Gordon Allport. 'On the contrary he develops defences. Like a dwarf in a world of giants, he cannot fight on equal terms. He is forced to listen to their derision and laughter and submit to their abuse.'

Attitudes within the family are important in other ways too. Studies have shown, for example, that adolescents from professional families are likely to grow up even more idealistic and liberal than their parents. They are also less prejudiced than children raised in families where the parents have a more conservative, pragmatic and 'business' orientated approach to life. The parents' level of education is another factor in the equation, with less prejudice being found among those who have received college training.

The child's sex is also significant, girls tend to be less prejudiced than boys and to express their hostility by ignoring those they dislike rather than treating them as inferiors. Religion too plays a part, with strongly religious adolescents tending to be less tolerant towards minorities than those who have little interest in religion. Personality is yet another element that must be considered, since well-adjusted children are generally less prejudiced. Indeed one seldom finds a deeply prejudiced person, adult or child, who does not also show some form of maladjustment, dependency needs, anxiety about status, guilt, sexual repression and so on, although these may not be consciously acknowledged.

Finally, the nature and intensity of any relationship with members of a minority group exert an influence not only over the growth of prejudice but also in its removal. While casual contact seldom brings about any changes of attitude, a more intimate involvement, especially between social or economic equals, reduces prejudice.

One of the earliest and best-known investigations into the growth of prejudice in children, was carried out by Muzafer and Carolyn Sherif in 1949. Twenty-four boys, aged around twelve, were selected from lower-middle-class Protestant American families. None of the group was friendly with any of the others, and all had similar educational backgrounds and attainments.

The children were taken to an isolated camp-site in northern Connecticut (the nearest town was eight miles away), and forbidden visitors. The experiment was conducted in three parts. At first all the boys were allowed to mix together and work on group activities around the camp. Maximum freedom was allowed in the choice of bunks, seats, friends and membership of teams for games. This was the 'friendship formation' part of the study, and most of the boys quickly made friends.

In the second stage, which the researchers called 'experimental in-group formation', the boys were directed to one of two teams, the Red Devils and the Bull Dogs. Members of each team were carefully chosen so that friends were deliberately separated.

Where a boy had made several friends he would be placed in the group which had the least number of them. Now a team spirit was generated by giving them tasks requiring co-operation; building a rope bridge, preparing food, organising a church service and so on.

In the final part of the experiment relationships between these two in-groups were studied by making the Red Devils and the Bull Dogs compete against one another in various activities: a tug-of-war, football and baseball games among others. The question which they wanted to answer, was whether the original friendships could survive the pressures of belonging to an in-group. When challenged to support their team or stand by an old friend, which choice would the boys make?

As predicted, they found that group influence outweighed the pull of former friendships. Both the Red Devils and the Bull Dogs developed a strong sense of solidarity and rigorously excluded members from the other team, even when they had once been friends.

In competitive or frustrating situations, hostility and the rudiments of stereotyped attitudes towards members of the out-group developed. When brought together in a relaxed atmosphere to eat a special meal, there was pandemonium as the teams scrapped and flung food around. Each team felt they were superior to the other and was prepared to fight to prove it. Before the boys were sent home, you may be relieved to learn, the psychologists reversed their attitudes yet again by devising activities in which the two teams co-operated together in tasks of mutual appeal to achieve a common goal, for instance they took part in a tug-of-war where boys pitted their collective strength against a steam-roller. By the time camp ended old friendships had been restored. But Sherif and Sherif had made their point. Prejudice can be created in young children with alarming ease.

Dislike, hostility and hatred are therefore learned responses which arise from all that a child sees, hears and experiences within the family, at school, and among his or her friends. The more closely allied they become to an in-group which holds aggressive attitudes towards other groups, the more likely they are to form friendships within that group and conform to its expectations.

On the more positive side, such attitudes can be reversed if people are allowed not merely to mix freely but to co-operate equally in tasks which interest everybody and benefit them all.

HOW TO BE HATED WITHOUT SAYING A WORD
So far we have looked at various aspects of dislike and hostility in terms of prejudice, since this is such a widespread cause of mutual loathing as well as being a widely researched topic in social psychology. When it comes to other causes of dislike, however, a different picture emerges. Surprisingly, for such an important topic, much less work has been done and much less is known about what makes Mr A dislike Mr B at first sight, or causes Mrs C to hate her new neighbour within moments of their meeting.

Intrigued by this dearth of scientific data Dr Jane Santo, of London University, decided to try and find out why people took a dislike to one another. She found that certain characteristics, such as an inability to laugh at oneself, coldness and a tendency to make others feel tense were common features of the generally disliked. Jane Santo then took her studies into psychiatric hospitals, since she felt that mental patients would be far more at risk of being consistently disliked by the world at large. Her hunch proved correct.

Medical students, for instance, rated their patients as much less likeable than other people, because they found their body language disturbing. Part of the distress created by these inappropriate silent speech messages may be due less to the things they do, such as making inappropriate gestures or unexpected facial expressions, as to their unintentional neglect of subtle non-verbal signals.

When two healthy individuals talk to one another, their bodies lock into an intricate and quite unconscious synchrony. Only when filmed in slow motion does the extent of this rhythmic interaction become apparent. As one person moves slightly foward another will move slightly back. A shift to the side may bring a mirror image response, a turn of the head result in the other person also turning his head. It happens even when two strangers are chatting together, but is likely to be far more obvious where intimate partners are involved.

We also send out signals to conduct conversations with the precision of an orchestra leader's baton. These unspoken messages indicate when we want to speak and the point at which we wish to stop talking and start listening. In part this is conveyed by changes in the voice, we allow it to drop prior to offering the other person a chance to contribute. But eye contact, posture and gesture are also used. If we want to carry on talking, for example, we'll probably avoid catching our listeners' eyes and may use an upward pointing finger to control any interruption on their part. This sharp movement, one observer described it as 'pricking the balloon of the other's attempt to speak,' is likely to be accompanied by a firm comment such as 'Just a moment . . .' or 'If you'll let me finish . . .'

When people fail to synchronise their postures, gestures, expressions and movements, with companions, those on the receiving end become distressed, although they may not always realise exactly why. It's a reaction that goes all the way back to babyhood, as experiments by Dr Colin Trevarthen at the University of Edinburgh have clearly shown. In this study, mothers talked to their babies through a special window. After a while the lighting was changed so that the face of a second adult was reflected onto the window, directly in front of the mother. She now began talking to this other grown-up who was, however, quite invisible to the infant. While chattering away to her baby, both mother and child synchronised their facial expressions. When she started her conversation with the adult, the mother shifted out of synchrony with the baby in order to synchronise with the silent speech signals of the adult. In no more than a few seconds, the baby became unsettled. So far as he, or she, was concerned 'Mum' was still talking to them and looking at them. Yet she was no longer responding to their signals. This distressed them so greatly that, usually within 30 seconds, they started to whimper and then cry.

It may be that when we dislike somebody, but can't really understand why, what actually distresses us is their inability to synchronise non-verbally and at a very basic level. Their macro-movements, smiles, nods, gestures may be perfectly appropriate but their microsignals, each lasting for only a fraction of a second, are discordant.

The use of eye-contact, for instance, is an extremely subtle and delicate business. Give too little and people are likely to regard you as devious, employ too much and they will interpret it – again not necessarily at a level of awareness – as a hostility signal.

That gaze alone can be interpreted as a threat was demonstrated in an intriguing experiment performed by Phoebe Ellsworth and her colleagues in 1972. Motorists were simply stared at as they waited for traffic lights to change and their levels of anxiety measured by the speed of their departure when the light changed green!

What I am suggesting, then, is that at least some cases of dislike could be caused by the other person unintentionally sending out body signals which disturb us either because they fail to synchronise with our own silent speech signals – in which case they presumably find talking to us equally unpleasant – or because signals are used inappropriately.

They stand too close, so invading our personal space and appear-ing to threaten our privacy, or too far way so that they seem emotionally as well as physically remote. They smile at the wrong moments, or fail to smile when expected. Their bodies remain stiff, signalling tension, in situations where we expect them to appear relaxed, so conveying an impression of not trusting us.

Alternatively they appear relaxed under circumstances where a certain amount of tension appears appropriate. For example I treated a child who had the unnerving habit of smiling whenever scolded or punished. As a result adults became increasingly angry and more punitive. They interpreted his smile as a sign of impu-dence. In fact it was a wholly inappropriate anxiety signal which the child had somehow acquired through learning. Because of the hostility the boy had experienced at the hands of teachers, and his own parents, he became seriously maladjusted. An important part of the therapy, therefore, was to help him to convey non-verbal signals more appropriate to his situation.

FRIEND OR FOE?

There are, of course, many other reasons why people may dislike one another. Some have already been considered when discussing prejudice and stereotypes. The way people look, or dress, wear their hair or use make-up, whether they have beards or glasses, their accents, the way they smell, even the places in which we meet them are just of a few of the multitude of clues which we appraise when making judgements about their probable personality and likely attitudes. If we approve of those imagined attitudes then we are predisposed to like them. If we disapprove then our initial judgements may be hostile or negative.

Our own moods and repressed anxieties also play a major role in deciding whether we will classify a stranger as potential friend or probable foe during first meetings. A male who is secretly concerned about his sexual orientation, for example, may feel threatened by somebody who appears to be a gay. A woman who feels herself to be rather unattractive might subconsciously resent any other woman who seems to be more beautiful.

If we are mellow and relaxed we are more likely to give people the benefit of the doubt and reserve final judgement until we know them rather better. Here an important and potent phenomenon called the 'halo' effect comes into play. If somebody is seen in elegant, high status surroundings, we are more likely to evaluate them positively than negatively. For example a scruffy old gent who might be dismissed as a tramp if seen in a rundown backstreet may appear impressively eccentric and interesting when observed leaving the lecture podium in a prestige university.

The extent to which people realise they are disliked is not always related to amount by which people actually dislike them, as Dr Jane Santo discovered during her researches. She feels that, in general, a great deal of our dislike for others is experienced below the level of everyday awareness because we feel uncomfortable about voicing such feelings. 'It's not until people are really pushed that they begin to say 'Hang on, I don't like this or that about them',' she explains.

Perhaps if we were willing to admit our own dislikes and prejudices to ourselves rather more openly, it might be easier to make friends instead of foes, and gradually to eliminate harmful social tensions. It is possible to reduce bigotry and end discrimination, some of the ways have been discussed in this chapter. But prevention is always better than cure and by acknowledging our own negative attitudes and stereotyped views we would be less likely to pass them onto the next generation. After all until hostility is admitted it remains inaccessible to reason and impossible to reduce.

The fact is that we are all, in our own way and to varying degrees, blinded by stereotypes and misled by prejudice. As Anatole France remarked: 'He flattered himself on being a man without any prejudices; and this pretension itself is a very great prejudice.'

9

I to I – an enigma solved?

> Each to each a looking glass,
> reflects the other that doth pass.

C. H. Cooley
Human Nature and the Social Order

After listening to a lengthy and learned argument on some obscure point of law, delivered by the eminent barrister and wit F. E. Smith (later Lord Birkenhead), a judge remarked sadly that he was, alas, 'none the wiser'.

'No wiser, my Lord,' retorted Frederick Edwin Smith majestically, 'but certainly better informed.'

At this point in the book you may be feeling rather like that unfortunate judge. I started by suggesting that the seemingly commonplace and commonsense experience of personal attraction actually presented a considerable enigma. I also demonstrated the extent to which a person is liked or disliked affects their educational attainments, treatment when ill, and hopes of escaping a guilty verdict in a court of law. In the chapters which followed, I explored some of the factors involved in both attraction and counter-attraction; the influence of looks, body size and shape, length of hair, style of dress, and body odours. The part played by biology in motherlove and frustration in prejudice have also been examined.

But, as you probably realise, a great many problems remain unsolved and even when answers have been offered some possess a disturbing tendency to take one around in circles.

For example, while it seems very likely that frustration causes people to seek out scapegoats, and stereotyping helps identify a minority group on whom bigoted people can vent their rage, not everybody who is frustrated and exposed to prejudicial propaganda allows herself, or himself, to be influenced. Many people resist every assault the State tries to make on their attitudes and, often openly and at great risk to themselves, resist the majority view. In Nazi-controlled Germany, for instance, even after years of virulent anti-semitic attacks, there remained a significant number of courageous and independent-minded Germans who were not taken in by Joseph Goebbels' brain-washing. They sheltered and tried to protect Jews. They formed an underground resistance to Hitler, and often paid for their opposition by a hideous and lonely death.

To take another point, in Chapter 2 I described how certain features of the male and female body seem to be preferred by certain personality types. Moderately built men with small chests, for instance, tend to attract women who have a more traditional view of the female role in society. Long-legged women are favoured by men who are less aggressive and more introspective than the majority of males. Assuming that these research findings are valid we are certainly better informed about the influence of personality over sexual attraction, but not really any wiser about why this should be so.

In this chapter therefore, I shall attempt to remedy these defects by proposing a new theory which focusses not on the objective realities of attraction but on each individual's subjective response to all that they see and hear, touch and smell. We shall concern ourselves less with what is happening in the outside world as with the patterns of thought and feeling going on inside our head.

A system of perception and assessment exists that is unique to each person and represents the sum total of life experiences up to each moment in time.

The starting point for this search for a more complete and satisfactory solution to the problem of personal attraction must, therefore, begin with our views not of others but of ourselves, since this self-image is central to our loving and loathing of others.

THE CONCEPT OF SELF

In the ancient Greek town of Phocis, at the foot of Mount

Parnassus, was temple sacred to Apollo in which resided the Dephic oracle. Carved on one wall of this building was the famous exhortation: 'Know thyself'. Down the centuries, a long line of poets, playwrights and novelists have echoed variations on this theme. Two thousand years later, Robert Burns was writing:

> Oh wad some power the giftie gie us
> to see oursels as ithers see us,
> It wad frae monie a blunder free us,
> An foolish notion.

Surprisingly, given this lengthy history of fascination with discovering just who we really are and what makes us tick, the term 'self-concept' was only invented in this century. Before then, ideas about the 'self' were inextricably bound up with metaphysical concepts such as the 'soul' or 'spirit' and so regarded as a subject for religious speculation rather than scientific investigation.

Man was seen as having a dual nature. There was body and there was soul, the one mortal, the other immortal; the former available to science, the latter beyond the reach of human reason.

Up to the 17th century, the concept of Self was closely allied to metaphysical notions of 'soul' and 'spirit', making open to ambiguity but closed to scientific investigation, views which had remained almost unchanged since the time of Plato and Homer, although the dichotomy between body and soul was most pronounced in the Christian religion. With the famous statement by the French mathematician and philosopher, René Descartes *Cogito ergo sum* (I think, therefore I am) there arrived a new dualism, subtly different from the old and much closer to 20th century thinking. It was a separation of content from consciousness which emphasised the central position of a self-concept in human awareness.

John Locke, an English philosopher, expanded on this idea by stressing the content of sensory experiences. Man, he believed, was a thinking, intelligent being 'that has reason and reflection and can consider self as itself.' Arguments supporting this view were put forward in the nineteenth century by the Scottish philosopher, David Hume. He pointed out that introspection always led to some particular perception or other: 'I never can catch myself at any time without a perception and never can observe anything but the perception.'

In his *Critique of Pure Reason*, the German philosopher Immanuel Kant distinguished between self as subject and self as object.

But it was not until the late nineteenth century that the American psychologist William James, elaborated this subject-object relationship. James severely criticised earlier philosophic beliefs linking self and soul, remarking that: 'The Soul is an outbirth of that sort of philosophising whose great maxim . . . is 'Whatever you are totally ignorant of, assert to be the explanation of everything else.'''

James's main contribution was to distinguish between self as knower and self as known: 'Our self feeling in this world,' he wrote, 'depends on what we back ourselves to be or do.' An insight which he used to create the ingenious formula:

$$\text{Self-esteem} = \frac{\text{Success}}{\text{Pretension}}$$

By this he meant that the way we feel about ourselves depends on the objective reality of actual attainment divided by the subjective notions of our goals and ambitions. These pretensions determine what roles, attributes, possessions and achievements will be seen as worth while and which are regarded as either less significant or entirely irrelevant.

James expressed this idea in the following way: 'I, who for the time have staked my all on being a psychologist, am mortified if others know much more psychology than I. But I am content to wallow in the grossest ignorance of Greek. My deficiencies there give me no sense of personal humiliation at all. Had I "pretensions" to be a linguist, it would have been just the reverse . . . Yonder puny fellow . . . whom everyone can beat, suffers no chagrin about it, for he has long ago abandoned the attempt to "carry that line", as the merchants say, of self at all. With no attempt there can be no failure; with no failure no humiliation. So our self-feeling in this world depends entirely on what we *back* ourselves to be and do.'

But the sense of self depends not only on the goals we set ourself in life, it is also affected by 'pretensions' that arise from obligations imposed by our culture, social class, family and peer group expectations. As Dr R. B. Burns says in his book *The Self-Concept*: 'Since man is a social animal and lives in society, he cannot avoid the social and cultural roles, values and norms stemming from this society. He finds himself judged by the criteria of his society and relevant subgroups, not merely those criteria of his own making.'

These are important ideas in our attempt to understand the truth about personal attraction, and we shall be returning to them in a moment.

WHAT SORT OF SELF?

Freud saw humankind as puppets manipulated by the instinctive drives of the Ego, Superego and the Id. John Broadus Watson and

152

Burrhus Frederick Skinner, the founders of the behaviourist school of psychology, also considered men and women to be victims of circumstance, this time driven not by subconscious drives but by the rewards (reinforcements) and punishments they had received.

By reinforcing some behaviours, their theory claimed, it is possible to get people, quite unknowingly, to act exactly as you wish. In one of the most vainglorious claims made by the behavioural school, Skinner once asserted that, given any infant, he could produce whatever kind of adult was desired: tinker, tailor, beggar-man or thief. According to this interpretation, remarks British psychologist Don Bannister, people become no more than a 'ping pong ball with a memory,' constantly batted to and fro by events beyond their control.

The theory favoured by Don Bannister, and the one I am proposing here as the most successful way of understanding the enigma of personal attraction, views humans in a very different light. No longer the victims of deep-rooted and frequently unconscious drives, no longer merely responding passively to rewards and punishments, men and women are viewed by this theory as being able to exert deliberate and effective control over their own destinies; of being self-determining agents of change rather than the helpless victims of circumstance; of acting through successful anticipation instead of reacting to unpredictable events.

PERSONAL CONSTRUCTS AND PERSONAL ATTRACTION
This refreshingly positive view of humans was developed during the Fifties by an American psychologist named George Alexander Kelly. Born in 1905, raised in Kansas and educated at the Friends University and Park College in Missouri, Kelly's graduate studies took him to Minnesota and Edinburgh universities, and he received his Ph.D. from the State University of Iowa in 1931.

Kelly was both a teacher and a clinical psychologist whose travelling clinic took him all over his home state. During the morning Kelly would teach, supervise students and concern himself with problems of education. In the afternoon he helped patients with a wide range of emotional and intellectual difficulties. Before very long, Kelly began to see that each of these seemingly different activities had a common thread. He realised that the way people felt towards others told you a great deal about the way they saw themselves.

If a teacher said a child was lazy, for instance, Kelly attempted to understand both the pupil's behaviour and the way the complaining teacher construed the idea of 'being idle'. For both student and adult might be, and very often were, looking at this idea or 'construct' of laziness in entirely different ways.

To see how Kelly's theory can help us become wiser about the enigma of personal attraction, we need to understand two essential ideas. The first is a philosophical view of the world known as *constructive alternativism*. The second, Kelly's analogy between the way people try to make sense out of the things that happen to them, and the approach of a researcher attempting to develop a scientific theory.

I will start by explaining the meaning of *constructive alternativism*, a cumbersome title for a delightfully simple notion, which appeals both to commonsense and common experience.

Imagine a miners' strike which has been dragging on for months and creating increasing bitterness. As some miners begin drifting back to work, fighting breaks out on the picket lines, people are injured and property damaged. Now put yourself in the position of an unbiased observer who goes around and interviews those involved. You'll agree that she, or he, is likely to hear a very different version of what happened when talking to striking miners, working miners, police officers, colliery managers, journalists and photographers. Assume for the moment that all those witnesses are being honest in their testimony and telling things as they saw them without intentionally embellishing their reports for political purposes. Even under these conditions, you'll agree that each account is likely to be very different.

Where then does the truth lie? The truth may well be that it doesn't reside anywhere. All are honest, but their stories differ because of the alternative constructions they place on events. Since each brings to that event a unique view of the world, the sum total of experience and training, each will not only focus on slightly different aspects of the encounter – a point which was made in the last chapter – but also interpret what is seen from a different subjective standpoint. For this reason alone there may never be any final agreement over what happened. As Dr Johnson once remarked on seeing two fishwives engaged in a furious row across the narrow alley separating their homes: 'I fear those ladies will never agree. They are arguing from different premises.'

This, then, was the view Kelly took as a result of his teaching and clinical experiences. Since there is no objective, absolute truth, the things which happen to us only make sense in terms of the constructions placed on them. Reality does not directly reveal itself to us, but can be construed in as many alternative ways as we are able to invent, a fact that explains the wide variety of human experience.

Since events do not carry their own meanings engraved on their backs, it has to be the ways in which we construe them which give them whatever significance they may have in relation to our own activities.

'Whatever nature may be, or howsoever the quest for truth will turn out in the end,' wrote Kelly, 'the events we face today are subject to as great a variety of constructions as our wits will enable us to construe. This is not to say that at some infinite point in time human vision will not behold reality out to the utmost reaches of existence. But it does remind us that all our present perceptions are open to question and reconsideration, and it does broadly suggest that even the most obvious occurrences of everyday life might appear utterly transformed if we were inventive enough to construe them differently.'

Notice the similarity between what Kelly said in 1955, and what William James wrote in 1860. How we feel about things, including success and failure, depends on the significance of those events in terms of our sense of self.

There was nothing especially original in this viewpoint which has been expressed, in various ways, by writers and philosophers down the centuries. The celebrated Stoic philosopher Epictetus commented in AD60: 'Man is disturbed not by things but the views he takes of them,' a view echoed by Shakespeare: 'There is nothing either good or bad, but thinking makes it so.'

The seventheenth-century English poet Alexander Pope was of the opinion that: 'All seems infected to th' infected spy, as all looks yellow to the jaundiced eye,' while Immanuel Kant observed that the only feature common to all mental disorders was the development by an individual of 'a unique private sense of reasoning'.

The essence of construct theory was also expressed by writers such as Paul Dubois: 'If we wish to change the sentiments it is necessary before all to modify the idea which produced them,' and therapists like Alfred Adler: 'It is very obvious that we are influenced not by "facts" but by our interpretation of them.'

How, then, do Kelly's ideas differ from the notions of earlier thinkers and ancient religious beliefs, for instance Buddhism, in which concepts similar to personal construct theory play an important role? The differences become more apparent when we take the second fundamental idea in his personal construct theory: that of people as scientists.

Working with subjects in psychological experiments, Kelly was struck by a paradox. There he was applying scientific method to exploring human emotions and motivations in an attempt to predict and control behaviour, yet failing to accept that his subjects approached life in an almost identical manner. As he later wrote: 'It is as though the psychologist were saying to himself, "I, being a psychologist and therefore a scientist, am performing this experiment in order to improve the prediction and control of certain human phenomena; but my subject, being merely a human organism, is obviously propelled by inexorable drives welling up within him, or else he is in gluttonous pursuit of sustenance and shelter."'

According to 'personal construct theory' this distinction is artificial and acts as a barrier to a proper understanding both of oneself and others.

How does the scientist set about her work? She starts with a general theory about the way things probably work and develops a specific hypothesis which is then tested by means of experiments. If the outcome is as expected, then the scientist has more reason to trust her theory and apply it in similar circumstances. It helps her by making outcomes more predictable. As more and more experiments support her theory, she is able to anticipate the course of events with increasing confidence and accuracy. An excellent example of this approach in action can be found in the way physician John Snow identified the true cause of cholera during the early nineteenth century. At that time cholera, a disease which killed many hundreds of people each year in Britain, was believed to be spread – in common with other infectious diseases – by the 'effluvia' given off in the breath of patients or from the corpses of victims and inhaled by a healthy person. There was a certain amount of evidence in favour of this theory, but Snow came to a different view. He believed that cholera was spread via water-borne infection. In 1849 a severe cholera epidemic swept through many square miles of streets and squares in central London. There were more than 500 fatalities in just a few streets alone. Snow then used his general theory about the way infectious diseases were spread to form a specific hypothesis. He believed that the source of the epidemic was sewage contaminated water drawn from a pump in Broad Street. His next step was to test his hypothesis by having the pump handle removed. The number of new cases of the disease dropped abruptly. Snow was then able to use his hypothesis to predict where other outbreaks of cholera were likely to occur.

The scientific method, by which events which previously seemed haphazard can be accurately and confidently predicted, has many similarities with the way people set about taking the chance out of everyday living.

First they develop a theory about the way things work, from this they form a specific hypothesis designed to help them anticipate the outcome of particular events. The hypothesis is then put to the test by behaving in a particular way and watching the outcome. If the results are as anticipated and desired, a person becomes more confident that his theory is valid. He, or she, is more likely to use the same approach in similar circumstances from then on to obtain a desired outcome, and to help exert control over an otherwise opaque and unpredictable future.

The infant in the nursery finds that loud bawling brings mother running. He develops a theory which says, 'If you want attention, cry.' He cries and the theory seems to work. Parents do pay attention: food, dry nappies and soothing words are the outcome. As he grows older, however, the child finds that this theory starts to break down. Crying at the baby-sitter brings only a harsh rebuke, crying in school results in ridicule from the other kids. At this point the child will probably modify his theory, crying for attention from parents but behaving in other ways when demanding attention from different adults.

But the infant's theory is not just about being comforted or fed. It is more an attempt to impose some kind of structure on a complex world, to devise ways in which events can be controlled in order that outcomes can be anticipated correctly. In the words of Salvatore Maddi, Professor of Psychology and Social Sciences at the University of Chicago, we each engage in 'a continual attempt to predict and control the events [we] experience'.

Take the case of Mr Smith who, as a result of all his experiences in life, the way he was brought up, the social class he has mixed with, the lessons he learned at school and university, and everything else which goes to make up his unique set of experiences, believes that if you are polite and friendly towards other people they will, more often than not, respond in a similar manner. So long as life works out as he anticipates, Mr Smith will continue to have confidence in his theory and use it as a means of making an uncertain future more predictable.

If his theory starts to let him down by failing to anticipate events successfully, a number of things may happen. Initially Mr Smith may become very anxious, or aggressive. After several failures he may try to modify his theory in various ways in order to protect himself from further distress. The implications of these changes for his liking, or loathing, of others will be explained in a moment.

An example helps make this clear. While driving to a New Year's party, Mr Smith reflects on what is likely to happen during the evening. On the basis of his theory and from experience of its success during previous parties, he anticipates that if he is relaxed, friendly and agreeable to other guests he'll have a good time, be liked and generally thought well of.

Now imagine that, unknown to him, a former girl-friend who hates his guts has spread the entirely false rumour that Mr Smith has served a jail sentence for child molesting. The other guests are horrified and decide to have nothing to do with him. Smith arrives, starts making friendly overtures to the first person he meets and is instantly and coldly rebuffed. Surprised and shocked he crawls away into a corner to lick his wounds and try to work out why the man was so hostile.

His theory allows for people not to respond to his friendly advances under certain circumstances, for example if they are drunk, or on drugs. He therefore explains his reception by telling himself the stranger was either an alcoholic or an addict. Reassured by this answer, Mr Smith makes another friendly overture to a different guest and is again rebuffed. After several such aggressive rejections, the unfortunate man becomes extremely distressed since his theory is completely failing to anticipate events.

Kelly suggested that such failures are the reason why people become anxious. When we no longer anticipate events successfully, in situations where we expected to make accurate predictions, he described the consequence as being caught 'with our constructs down'. The same thing would happen in the scientific community if some theory in which people had great confidence suddenly began to make inaccurate predictions. There would be surprise that events once efficiently anticipated by the theory were no longer capable of prediction.

Now we'll let Mr Smith off the hook by having his penitent girl-friend stand up and admit that it was all a lie designed to teach him a lesson. Everybody is very apologetic and embarrassed. They do their best to make up to him for the boorish conduct to which he was subjected.

With the mystery solved Mr Smith may feel only a sense of relief that his theory is valid after all and failed only because of an exceptional and probably never to be repeated circumstance. On the other hand he may well feel more than a little peeved that people should be prepared to accept such slanders so easily, and hurt that somebody he was once fond of could try to hurt him so badly. Both these new insights might well cause him to modify his theory in various ways, perhaps by making him less trusting or more cynical.

By providing an intentionally simple example, I may have given the impression that construct theory is a rather simple-minded way of looking at the enormous complexities of human emotions and relationships. In fact it is an extremely involved and sophisticated way of exploring the inner world of feelings and one which has found wide application in many fields of psychology.

For one thing we always hold and apply our theories within a constant interaction between ourselves and others. Their expectancies depend mainly on their understanding of us, which means that what we do often depends on what we believe other people expect us to do based on their particular construction of us. They in turn respond to their expectations of our expectations of them, and so on.

Turn this notion around in your mind for a moment and you'll realise just how complicated the whole process can become. One is reminded of a poem by R. D. Laing from his book *Knots*, in which he confided:

> They are playing a game. They are playing at not
> playing a game. If I show them I see they are,
> I shall break the rules and they will punish me
> I must play their game, of not seeing I see the game

What is more, our example of Mr Smith and his response to the other guests' rudeness gave the impression that an individual's theory consists of just one of two constructs, or ways of looking at the world. In his case these would have been the constructs of 'politeness' and 'friendliness' but nothing else.

In real life, of course, our theories consists of many, many more constructs – or ways of looking at life – which will be related to each other in a variety of ways.

By identifying an individual's major constructs and working out how these fit together to create a unique model of personal reality it becomes possible to gain deep insights into the nature of his theories and so discover, among many other things about him, the sort of people he will like and dislike. To understand how this can be done, I need first to explain more both about the nature of constructs and Kelly's personal construct theory.

CONSTRUCTS IN ACTION

Constructs are simply ways of making distinctions between things. The things (Kelly called them Elements and I shall do the same) can be other people, animals, places, situations, events or objects. In fact they can be anything in the world.

If we say, 'Soap A smells more antiseptic than soap B,' or, 'Mrs T is further to the right politically than Mr B', we are using the constructs 'smells of antiseptic – does not smell of antiseptic'; and 'right wing – left wing' to distinguish between them.

A construct, then, is a way in which two or more elements are seen as being alike and yet different from other things. It is a way of making sense of the world in order to anticipate outcomes. By using soap A, for instance, we anticipate killing more germs than by using soap B. By voting for Mrs T we anticipate a more conservative approach to social problems than if we give our vote to Mr B.

But it must always be borne in mind that constructs are simply useful inventions, they are never an intrinsic part of the elements being contrasted. As Kelly expressed it, each one of us 'erects a structure, within the framework of which substance takes shape or assumes meaning. The substance which he construes does not produce the structure; the person does.'

That is to say, elements never tell us what they are, how they are or why they are. This we must discover for ourselves and the instrument of enquiry is our personal system of constructs.

You may have noticed that the constructs described above come in pairs, Kelly called them 'poles' – 'smells antiseptic – does not smell of antiseptic'; 'right wing – left wing'. All constructs are regarded as possessing two such poles, since one cannot, for example, know what it means to be 'intelligent' without also having an idea of what it means not to be 'intelligent'. The opposing poles of a construct should be thought of in terms of contrasts. For instance, the opposite pole of 'sweet' would be 'sour', rather than 'not sweet', just as the contrasting pole of 'bass' is 'treble' and 'acid' is 'alkaline' rather than 'not bass' and 'not acid'. This division into contrasting poles is, actually, fundamental to the way human's perceive the world. In the words of the author of *Small is Beautiful*, Ernst Schumacher: 'The nature of our thinking is such that we cannot help thinking in opposites . . . what matters is the tool-box of ideas with which, by which, through which, we experience and interpret the world.'

George Kelly's idea, then, is that each of us possesses a unique system of personal constructs that allow us to make sense of and anticipate events. This system shapes our thoughts, emotions and actions when confronting a world that would otherwise be almost impossible to understand.

Some people have complicated systems and can be more discriminating in their anticipation and interpretation of events. Others have rather simple systems which cause them to see life more in terms of black and white than in shades of grey. The more constructs people have in common the more they will perceive life in a similar way and the easier it will be for them to understand each other.

Equally the greater the differences in their construct systems the more individual they will be and the harder it will be for them to find any common ground.

Constructs are, as I have explained, acquired through experience and can be modified. But some are more easily altered than others since they are arranged in a hierarchy with those higher up the ladder being less readily changed than others. The hierarchy also means that high-level constructs can exert control over those below them.

For instance a person might have a construct which told him it was wrong to kill people. But if he also had a higher-level construct which said it was right to obey orders in defence of his country, he would probably be able to kill without much guilt in times of war. Or to take a less dramatic example, for some people the construct *good jazz* versus *modern jazz* could come under the constructs of *good jazz* versus *bad jazz* while both might be subsumed under the music pole *music* versus *noise*. Some people are more flexible in their ability to change or modify constructs than others. A feature of paranoid men and women, for example, is that their constructs tend to be inflexible and cannot be changed to deal with changed circumstances.

EXPLORING CONSTRUCTS

One of the features which makes Kelly's theory so interesting and helpful is that it can be used as the starting-point for a complex analysis of individual construct systems. This, as I have already mentioned, often yields extremely valuable insights into the way people feel about others, their self-image and outlook on life.

The first step is to identify some of their more important constructs, that is those which are high up in the system and so exert significant influence on less potent constructs below them.

There are a number of methods for eliciting constructs from people, but an effective and widely used approach is known as 'laddering'. Devised by an American psychologist Dr D. Hinkle, it allows the investigator to move upwards through a person's systems, each question revealing a construct a rung or so higher on the 'ladder'. The procedure works as follows. An individual is asked to write down the names of several people he, or she, knows well – father, mother, brothers and sisters, husband or wife, friends and close relatives, people at work and so on. These are usually noted on individual cards which can then be rearranged into various sequences.

This done, the next task is to choose three of the names, selecting them in such a way that two of the people picked have something in common which distinguishes them from the third. For example, having selected his mother, father and best friend, the subject might explain this choice by saying that while his mother and best friend were very warm people emotionally, his father was rather a cold person.

The name cards are swopped around in order to pick out as many similarities and differences as possible. When this task is completed the person carrying out the analysis, usually a psychologist, selects one of the constructs – here it might be 'emotionally warm – emotionally cold', and asks which is preferred.

If the choice is for 'warm', the subject is then asked to explain why, and the conversation which follows might go like this:

Subject: 'Because warm people find it easier to make friends.'
Psychologist: 'What I would like to understand now is why you feel it important to make friends.'
Subject: 'That way you have people to confide in.'
Psychologist: 'So what advantages do you see in confiding in others?'
Subject: 'Talking your problems over helps get them clear in your head.'
Psychologist: 'I understand that, but can you tell me why it's important to see problems clearly?'
Subject: 'Otherwise you might make a bad mistake.'
Psychologist: 'What might happen if you made a bad mistake?'
Subject: 'Somebody could get hurt when you didn't mean it to happen.'

As you can see 'laddering' allows the hierarchy of constructs to be explored, with each new construct identified being more important than those below it. Starting from the construct pair of 'warm – cold', we next discovered that 'warmth' was linked to the constructs of 'having friends – not having friends' while this, in turn, was subordinated to the idea of 'confiding – not being able to confide' and so on. The construct 'hurting – not hurting' people was the most important construct elicited in the discussion, although there could well have been higher order constructs which would have been identified by further questioning. Eventually a point will be reached where there are no further rungs on the ladder and we have arrived at one of that person's 'core constructs', so called because it lies at the very centre of their sense of self.

I should caution that 'laddering' is a very powerful psychological technique which can produce severe emotional distress if used incorrectly.

Once constructs have been elicited, they may – if desired – be given a number value. One way is to rank them in order of importance for each of the people whose names were written on the card.

Another method is to rate them on a scale of, say, 1–7, where 1 would mean that it applied very strongly to a particular individual, while a rating of 7 meant that it did not apply at all. The person whose constructs were being analysed would then be asked to rate all his, or her, constructs for each name on the card.

Here's how the final result might appear. It explores the construct system of a 22-year-old man called Martin. On the chart are the ratings he gave to seven people, the elements, on six constructs. You'll notice that two of the elements are Martin as he sees himself right now, and how he hopes to be in the future.

MARTIN'S CONSTRUCT RATINGS

Constructs	Elements						
	Dad	Mum	Sister	Brother	Best Friend	Me/ now	Me/ later
Clever	1	5	2	2	5	2	4
Warm	7	2	5	4	2	6	1
Friendly	6	1	5	5	2	5	1
Tolerant	5	2	4	5	1	6	2
Jealous	2	6	3	2	5	3	6
Relaxed	7	2	2	4	2	6	2

Bearing in mind that on the scale used to make these ratings, 1 = very true and 7 = not true at all, certain similarities and differences between the seven people concerned become apparent simply by studying the chart.

For instance, Martin sees his mother and father as having different personalities, at least so far as these six attributes are concerned, since their ratings are dissimilar. Dad he regards as clever, but very cold emotionally, fairly intolerant, quite jealous and not at all relaxed. Mum, by comparison, is not seen as especially bright, but she is certainly warm, friendly, tolerant, not especially jealous and very relaxed.

Now if you look at how Martin sees himself at this moment, you'll immediately notice that the ratings are much nearer those of his father than his mother. Martin doesn't seem to like this situation much, however, since his ambition is to become more like his mother – the 'Me/later' ratings are close to those he gave her on all the constructs.

Martin views his brother and sister as like one another, and closer to their father than their mother. The only exception is the rating for the construct of 'relaxed', where his sister is seen as being a good deal less uptight than his brother.

While such an 'eyeball' analysis is instructive and provides some useful clues about the kind of people Martin seems likely to find attractive (look how similar the ratings for 'best friend' are to 'Mum' and how different they are from Dad's scores) there is much more information to be gleaned from a more sophisticated analysis of the chart. This, you may not be too surprised to learn, means a mathematical analysis.

To make sense of the discussion that follows it's necessary to have some knowledge of a statistical measure called the *correlation*, which means taking a brief, but not alarming, detour through the world of numbers. If you are already familiar with these ideas then please skip the next section.

THE MEANING OF CORRELATIONS

Suppose we measured the heights and weights of twenty men and found that as height increased so did weight – not a very remarkable discovery. These findings would show that height was positively correlated with weight. The shortest man was the lightest, the next tallest the next heaviest and so on right up to the tallest man who was also the heaviest.

Now imagine that we compared their annual income with height and weight. Here, under normal circumstances, it would be strange if we found any significant relationship, or correlation, between the two. Unless you are a bar-room bouncer, all-in wrestler or lumber-jack, height and weight probably have little influence on how much you earn. In other words salary level and body build are independent of one another.

Finally, let's see what happens if we give those men two psychological tests, the first assessing their level of maturity and the second the amount of frustration each is able to tolerate before flying into an infantile rage. We would find that the better adjusted they were, the less likely it was that frustration would lead to temper tantrums. In this case there would be an inverse relationship, or negative correlation, between these aspects of their personality.

Positive correlations, of the kind described in the first part of our example, are measured on a scale of $0 - +1$. The higher the number the closer the relationship, the lower the number the less they are associated. In fact a correlation of zero means that there is no relationship at all between those two items on that variable. In the height-weight measure we might find a correlation as high as 0.8 or

164

0.9, although in real life it would never be a perfect positive correlation of +1.

Income and stature, since they are not related, would have a theoretical correlation of 0.

Negative correlations, of the sort described in the last part of the example where as maturity increases outbursts of infantile rage decrease, one goes up, the other goes down, are measured on a scale of $0 - -1$. The relationship between maturity and infantile rage reactions might be around -0.75 or higher, although once again it would not be a perfect (-1) correlation.

One final point to bear in mind is that correlation does not imply causation. Because there is a positive or negative relation between two items you cannot say that one produces the other. For instance there is a positive correlation between the number of storks seen in Switzerland and the number of babies born. Equally, there is a negative correlation between the number of people with a Ph.D. in any American state and the number of mules found. In each case the relationship is explained by a third event, where storks and babies are concerned this is the arrival of spring, while for Ph.D.'s and mules it's simply that high tech states attract more Ph.D.s than farmers. This is an important consideration to keep in mind when studying the construct analysis which follows. Because there is, for example, a high positive correlation between being *clever* and being *jealous* does not mean that cleverness causes jealousy or the other way around!

Similarly a high negative correlation, say between being *clever* and being *tolerant*, does not imply that it's tolerance which prevents that person from having a high IQ.

ANALYSING MARTIN'S CONSTRUCTS
There are many ways of analysing a chart like Martin produced, which results from ranking or rating constructs against elements. You can, for example, take a pocket calculator and simply work out all the correlations using the procedures described in the Appendix.

This is time-consuming and tedious but not at all difficult. On the other hand it is far easier to use one of several computer programmes to do the work for you. Some are so complicated, and perform such a sophisticated analysis, that you need a main-frame to run them and a great deal of knowledge and experience to interpret them. Others are far more user-friendly, can be run on a micro-computer and provide a print-out which is reasonably easy to understand.

The numbers on Martin's grid have been crunched on a micro-computer using a programme which correlates all the constructs and all the elements, and then ranks those constructs and elements in order of importance using a technique we need not go into here. What matters, so far as understanding the way construct analysis helps us solve the puzzle of attraction, is what the printout says.

We'll begin by looking at Martin's constructs to see what relationships they have to one another.

RELATIONSHIPS BETWEEN CONSTRUCTS ON MARTIN'S CHART

Constructs		Constructs			
	Warm	Friendly	Tolerant	Jealous	Relaxed
Clever	−0.90	−0.95	−0.91	0.92	−0.76
Warm		0.94	0.87	−0.88	0.84
Friendly			0.89	−0.98	0.75
Tolerant				−0.86	0.80
Jealous					−0.72

Notice, that we don't correlate Clever with Clever, or Warm with Warm since this relationship will clearly be 1 in every case.

Also, only half the chart needs to be written out since all the figures below the diagonal will simply be a mirror image of those above the diagonal, as a moment's thought will make clear. For instance, the correlation between warm and friendly is obviously identical to the correlation between friendly and warm. This kind of matrix takes a few moments to get used to, but you will find it quite simple to read and understand if you follow the instructions below.

Let's start by moving from left to right across the top line to see what it means to Martin if he construes somebody as 'clever', and how this assessment is going to influence his liking or disliking.

The first number we come to, under the heading 'warm' is a high negative correlation −0.90. Remember that if it had been −1 there would have been a perfect *negative* correlation between those two constructs in Martin's way of looking at life.

As it is the strength of this negative relationship implies that Martin will regard clever people as lacking warmth; nor will he consider them either friendly (−0.95) or tolerant (−0.91).

They will, however, be viewed as 'jealous' since at 0.92 this is a strong *positive* correlation – where there is no sign in front of the number you take it to be a positive correlation.

So people Martin considers clever people are also going to possess a great many negative qualities, and he may find it hard to like them purely for this reason.

Now let's take the next construct on the left-hand column, 'warm' to see how this relates to Martin's other constructs. We have already seen how 'warm' and 'clever' go together, so the first pair to consider is warm with friendly. Here we find a strong positive correlation of 0.94. Martin sees friendly people as warm and warm people as friendly. He also sees them as being tolerant (0.87) and – missing out jealousy for a moment – relaxed (0.84). They are not, however, jealous people since there is a high negative correlation (−0.88) between these two constructs.

Warm people, in Martin's view, are therefore going to be friendly, relaxed and tolerant but never jealous. This suggests that if Martin is friendly with somebody who unexpectedly displays a jealous streak he may well start to see him, or her, in a much more negative way.

Armed with this information it should be easy for you to reach your own conclusions about the way the remaining four constructs of friendly, tolerant, jealous, and relaxed go together.

The computer also worked out which constructs were most important to Martin and the order in which he placed them. This showed that being friendly and relaxed were very important to him and shaped the way he anticipated events. When introduced to somebody who seemed relaxed, for instance, Martin would form a favourable impression and predict that he would also find him friendly.

Before looking at other ways of presenting the information contained in the table above, let's explore the way in which the seven people on the chart relate to one another. Once again the figures below represent positive or negative correlations.

RELATIONSHIPS BETWEEN PEOPLE ON MARTIN'S CHART

Elements			Elements			
	Mum	Sister	Brother	Best Friend	Me/Now	Me/Later
Dad	−0.89	0.51	0.81	−0.87	0.94	−0.85
Mum		−0.58	−0.95	0.93	−0.86	0.97
Sister			0.64	−0.55	0.50	−0.59
Brother				−0.96	0.86	−0.87
Best Friend					−0.95	0.87
Me/Now						−0.79

Let's start, as before, by working from left to right to see, first of all, how Martin construes his father. As we realised by simply comparing the ratings visually, Dad and Mum are not seen as very alike.

This is confirmed by the high negative (−0.89) correlation which the computer has calculated. Martin does, however see his father as somewhat like his sister (0.51) and much more like his brother (0.81) since both these correlations are positive. His father and his best friend are very dissimilar (−0.87) but Martin sees himself *now* as very much like his father, (0.94), closer to him than either his sister or his brother in fact. However he hopes, in the future, to be very much less like his father (−0.85).

Martin sees his mother as not like either his sister (−0.58) his brother (−0.95) or himself as he is now (−0.86). She is, however, a lot like his best friend (0.93) and very much the way he hopes to be in the future (0.97).

Before leaving this matrix of correlations, and allowing you to explore the other relationships in Martin's life, let us consider how he regards his best friend. This time it will probably be easier to work down the column headed 'Best Friend'. We have already looked at the relationship between best friend/father and best friend/mother. Now it is clear that his best friend is like neither his sister (−0.55) nor especially, his brother (−0.96).

To discover out how closely Martin identifies with his best friend, we need to work along the row from the left hand column. This shows us a high negative correlation (−0.95) between Martin as he sees himself at the moment and his best friend. But, in the future, he hopes to be able to be much more like this friend (0.87).

When looking at the remaining correlations check to see how the extent to which Martin identifies himself as he is now with the way he hopes to be in the future.

As with the constructs on Martin's chart, the computer kindly works out which of the people in his life are most important to him. These turn out to be his *mother* and his *best-friend*.

If you are one of those people whose head reels at the sight of figures, especially when they include a decimal point, you may be feeling more than a little confused by this time. If so, the diagram overleaf (Figure 1) should help make matters clear.

Here the rather off-putting rows of decimals have been given a friendlier face by transforming them into a map which gives us a clearer impression of how Martin views those seven people in his life. I'll explain how you can create a similar map of your own people and constructs in the Appendix.

On the map, two of the seven people his brother and his sister, have been placed at each end of two crossed lines. These people were chosen because the analysis showed them as being of great significance in Martin's life. How you work this out is explained in the Appendix.

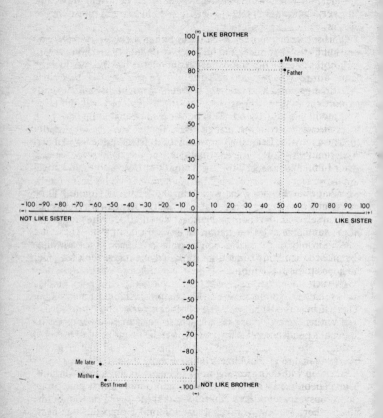

The remaining five people are located on the mental map according to their relationships with Martin's brother and sister, relationships identified by the correlation table. As you can see this clearly illustrates the main points already discussed. Martin sees his father as being like 'me now', and like his brother and sister. His mother, best-friend and himself as he expects, or hopes, to become are very unlike his brother, his sister, his father and himself as he is now.

This suggests that he is most likely to find attractive people who are unlike brother, sister and father, but have more in common with his mother – which is almost certainly one of the things which he finds attractive about his best friend. We can also see that since Martin hopes to change, and become more like those he finds attractive, there is a sharp distinction between the Ideal Self (represented by Me Later) and Real Self (represented by Me Now).

As I explained in the first chapter, friends may be chosen not because they are like us – Martin obviously doesn't see himself and his friend as having much in common at present – but because they fulfill the role of bridging the gulf between Real and Ideal Self.

What qualities will Martin find attractive? Clearly there will be many more attributes than were included in this analysis. But, since Martin selected them, the six we have identified probably represent important factors in his liking or disliking of others. These are shown in Figure 2 overleaf. Once again two of the construct have been used to provide labels for the crossed line, while the remainder are positioned according to their relationship with these key constructs.

We have already identified the relationships between the constructs, but as with the association between people, this way of presenting the results makes it easier to get immediate impression of what's going on in Martin's mind when he forms an impression of others.

The constructs of being 'Relaxed' and 'Friendly' are closely related, in Martin's view of life, to being 'Warm' and 'Tolerant'. Clever people, however, are viewed as unfriendly, tense, and prone to jealousy. It seems likely, therefore, that Martin's best friend, like his mother, are warm, relaxed and tolerant individuals whom he does not regard as especially clever. His father, brother, sister and he himself at present, are probably perceived as clever, tense and not very friendly.

I must emphasise that these are not 'truths' about the people in Martin's life, merely the way they seem through his window on the world. Somebody else, for instance, might consider his best-friend

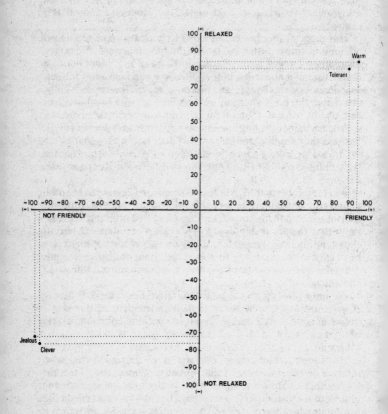

very bright, his father very relaxed and his mother very jealous. Such a divergence of views is only to be expected within the framework of constructive alternativism.

So far as attraction is concerned, it seems likely that Martin will find a clever person less agreeable than one he construes as having a lower IQ, not because he is prejudiced against intelligence in itself but because of the expectations – unfriendly, jealous and tense – this construct arouses in his mind.

What does all this tell us, about Martin's personal preferences when making friends and more usefully, about the ways in which people in general are attracted to one another?

First we have an explanation of why opposites may attract. Martin doesn't see himself in the least like his friend, rather he admires him for positive qualities which he feels he lacks, but hopes one day to possess. Part of the reason for his friendship may, indeed, be that it provides him with a role model whose envied response to life can be copied.

If the best friend feels equally attracted to Martin, we can assume that he admires those very qualities which Martin dislikes and hopes to change. Since the father and son seem similar in many ways, at least so far as Martin is concerned, it seems reasonable to suppose his best friend will like Martin's dad much more than Martin does, while possibly liking his mother rather less. This is largely speculation since we would need to explore the construct system of Martin's best friend in order to reach any firm conclusions. We might also suspect that the more Martin becomes likes his best friend, the greater the strains imposed on that friendship since their mutual attraction probably lies in those differences.

The message of Kelly's theory and this chapter, then, is that to understand attraction we must first understand the constructs a person uses to make sense of the world and anticipate likely outcomes.

Without this knowledge it becomes almost impossible to solve the puzzle of loving and loathing. There will, of course, be occasions when we do think we understand why two people attract or repel one another. When this happens it is because we share many constructs with them and so see the world from rather similar viewpoints. If we are baffled by their choice of a partner, or mystified by their friendships, we can assume that a lack of shared constructs prevents us from seeing those people as they do.

Since constructs are both acquired and modified by experiences, they change with time, causing us to view the world differently and so see old friends (who will also have changed in some ways) in a different light. Such changes may make friendships warmer and intimate relationships more loving. Equally they may start to distance us from people we were once close to.

In order to live happy, well-adjusted and fulfilling lives which include successful relationships with others, we need to develop a construct system that is capable of changing with changing circumstances, and sufficiently complicated to differentiate between people in subtle ways – rather than seeing them in stark, uncompromising terms.

The extent to which such a system evolves depends to a very great extent on childhood experiences. Those constructs of Martin's – and they were, of course only a very small part of his total construct system – which we analysed did not suggest a very happy relationship with his parents or with his current sense of self. In fact Martin seems a rather unhappy and unsettled individual.

If you are interested in exploring your own construct system, I provide two different methods for doing this in the Appendix: only one of them requires any serious calculations.

AN ENIGMA SOLVED?

I believe that Kelly's theory of personal constructs offers a way of explaining many of the reasons why people come to like or loathe one another. It may not provide all the answers we seek, nor offer a complete solution, but it does allow us to look at relationships in a refreshing and revealing new way.

Instead of focusing on outward reality, the theory suggests that we turn inward and explore the mental models we create of that reality. It encourages us to recognise that there is no absolute truth about events, including relationships, only a construction which we place on what happens: a construction with many equally valid alternatives. Martin saw his father as clever, but cold, unfriendly, intolerant, jealous and tense. He considered his mother as being just the opposite. But these are not final verdicts on either, they are simply the way Martin has come to view them through the window of his current set of constructs. They provide the means by which he anticipates how each parent will respond to him.

As Martin changes, perhaps grows more towards the kind of person he hopes to become in the future, this relationship with his parents will certainly alter. Perhaps at that point he will construe them quite differently, possibly seeing his mother's friendly tolerance as a form of dependency and his father's aloof coldness in terms of shyness and a lack of confidence. Such changes in outlook could bring with them a greater warmth towards his father and a distancing of himself from his mother.

Constructs, then, are dynamic and not static. Some change quite easily and quickly, although others – our core constructs – are far more resistant to change.

In situations where our constructs seem no longer adequate to anticipate events – as in the case of Mr Smith – we are likely to become anxious or hostile. Anxious because we no longer know how to cope. Aggressive as we try to force our outward reality to conform to our anticipated outcome in the face of contradictory evidence. Like the drunk who becomes more and more abusive and insistent when others decline to have a drink with him.

This girl will love me, a man tells himself, because his construct system is such that he anticipates women find him irresistible. If one doesn't he may then become angry and aggressive in an attempt to impose by force what he cannot achieve in any other way – the validation of a prediction.

To say that attraction depends on the particular construct system each individual has developed is not to rule out biological mechanisms. The role of early bonding, and the part played by odour are not ignored in this theory but merely seen as factors in an extraordinarily complex and constantly changing equation.

Loving or loathing depends on an interplay of constructs which are the product of cultural values, social expectations and – above all – early childhood during which many of our core constructs are formed.

THE CHALLENGE OF CHILDHOOD

A Beatles' song asks where all the lonely people come from. The answer, of course, is that they come from people just like us. People who, for a wide variety of reasons, either lack the opportunities or – more usually – the mental skills needed to make friends, attract lovers, develop lasting and comfortable relationships. The message of this chapter is that such failures are due not to any inborn and irredeemable flaws in their natures, but simply the result of unhelpful or inadequate constructs. Their ways of anticipating the events are such that they make it hard for them to get close to people. Instead they keep them at a distance, respond coldly to tentative advances, reject expressions of emotion, shun the desire to love and be loved by return. Anticipations which might come under this heading include:

'If I am not loved by everybody I am loved by nobody.'
'To love is to risk hurt and that must be avoided at all costs.'
'I will be rejected if I make the first advance.'
'Nobody attractive could ever find me attractive.'

174

The challenge of childhood is to help each child grow in such a way that these constructs – and others which prove equally damaging – never become part of the way they view the world. While there can be no formula by which this may be achieved, this poem by an anonymous writer comes very close to suggesting the best way of meeting the challenge.

> If a child lives with criticism
> He learns to condemn
> If a child lives with hostility
> He learns to fight
> If a child lives with ridicule
> He learns to be shy
> If a child lives with shame
> He learns to feel guilty
> If a child lives with tolerance
> He learns to be patient
> If a child lives with encouragement
> He learns confidence
> If a child lives with praise
> He learns to appreciate
> If a child lives with fairness
> He learns justice
> If a child lives with security
> He learns to have faith
> If a child lives with approval
> He learns to like himself
> If a child lives with acceptance and friendship
> He learns to find love in the world.

Appendix

Exploring your own constructs

As I have identified constructs as holding the key that unlocks the secrets of personal attraction, you may well feel sufficiently intrigued to explore your own feelings using the approach outlined in the last chapter. Here are two methods, the first having the advantage of involving no maths, the second requiring some calculations.

METHOD ONE

STEP ONE
Take eight small pieces of paper, number them 1 to 8, and write on each the name of someone who matches the descriptions below.
Sheet 1
'Somebody I love.'
Sheet 2
'Somebody I hate.'
Sheet 3
'A friend whose company I enjoy.'
Sheet 4
'A person I dislike being with.'
Sheet 5
'My father' (or the dominant male figure in your childhood).
Sheet 6
'My mother' (or the dominant female figure in your childhood).
Sheet 7
'Me now.'
Sheet 8
'Me as I expect (or hope) to be later'

STEP TWO
Select any three of those cards and identify some feature which two of them share but that is absent from the third.

You may realise, for instance, that you feel confident and relaxed

176

with your father (5) and someone you love (1), but tense and uncertain in the company of somebody you dislike (4).

Write this similarity and difference on a copy of the Analysis Chart shown opposite. Figure 1.

In the example above, you would write 'Make me feel confident' under the heading *These Two People Are Alike Because* and, 'Makes me feel unsure of myself' under the heading *This Person Is Different Because*.

Identify up to 8 similarities and differences by using the names in different combinations. Try to ensure that all of them are used, at least once, in the analysis.

STEP THREE

Investigate similarities and differences on the Analysis Chart, by asking yourself:

'Which of these feelings do I like the most?' When you have decided place a tick against that line on the chart, and a cross against the opposing feeling. For instance, if you enjoyed feeling 'confident' rather than 'uncertain' you'd tick the left side of the Chart against 'your father and the person you are in love with' and write a cross against 'the individual you dislike being with.'

Be honest with yourself when making this choice. If, for instance, you being 'uncertain of yourself' is rather exciting and challenging then tick this feeling and put a cross against 'feel confident.'

STEP FOUR

Now for the final step which explores the actual qualities that make you like or dislike others. Take two new sheets of paper and head them – *Like* and *Loathe*.

On the *Like* sheet write down all the points you ticked off on the Analysis Chart.

On your *Loathe* sheet note all the features with a cross against them on the Analysis Chart.

Study each in turn, starting with those on the *Like* sheet and expand the list by working out just what makes those characteristics attractive. Then do the same for your *Loathe* list, exploring why certain aspects of somebody's personality or appearance makes them unattractive to you.

If you feel up to some simple basic arithmetic, nothing more demanding than addition and subtraction is required, those lists can form the basis of a slightly more scientific analysis.

All you have to do is give each attribute a score from 1 to 20. All those on the *Like* being given a plus (+) value, and all those on the *Loathe* list receive a minus (−) value.

ANALYSIS CHART

THESE TWO PEOPLE ARE ALIKE BECAUSE:	THIS PERSON IS DIFFERENT BECAUSE:

Figure 1. Analysis chart for exploring your own constructs.

A feature on the *Like* list you regard as highly attractive could get a score of + 18 or even + 20, for instance, while a moderately attractive item might be scored + 8 or + 12. Similarly the least attractive feature on the *Loathe* list might merit a score of − 18 or − 20, while a less unattractive quality could be scored at − 5 or − 10.

Select somebody you have recently met and try to identify the 'Like' and 'Loathe' features of their appearance and personality. Add up the score for all the 'Like' features, then total up the 'Loathe' score and subtract one from the other. The number which remains is their Attraction Value.

As you will realise this is a lighthearted way of identifying and analysing constructs which has more entertainment value than scientific merit, although it can produce unexpectedly rewarding and helpful insights. However, if you would like to carry out a rather more advanced type of analysis and are not deterred by the prospect of some reasonably simple maths, you may like to work through the

ANALYSIS CHART

THESE TWO PEOPLE ARE ALIKE BECAUSE:	THIS PERSON IS DIFFERENT BECAUSE:
WARM ✓	COLD ✗
CLEVER ✓	DIM ✗
LOGICAL ✗	INTUITIVE ✓
SYMPATHETIC ✓	ALOOF ✗
SOCIABLE ✗	LONER ✓
TRUTHFUL ✓	DEVIOUS ✗
HONEST EMOTIONALLY	HIDES EMOTIONS ✓
GENEROUS ✓	MEAN ✗
SOPHISTICATED ✗	INNOCENT ✓
SELFISH ✗	GIVING ✓
AMBITIOUS ✗	PREFERS QUIET LIFE ✓
SUCCESSFUL ✓	FAILURE ✗

Figure 2. Example of completed Analysis chart.

second method provided. In this task you'll be greatly helped by a calculator.

METHOD TWO

1: PEOPLE
Copy out the Chart opposite Figure 3 to avoid marking this book. Against the descriptions in the column at the left-hand side of the Chart write in the initials of eight people who match the descriptions provided. You can, if you prefer, use alternative descriptions in order to include different people, but the formula provided is based on there being eight subjects on the Chart.

Any less, or any more, and you must modify part of this formula as described below.

Construct Analysis Chart

People	Constructs										
Somebody I love											
Somebody I hate											
Friend like being with											
Person dislike being with											
My father											
My mother											
Me as I am now											
Me I as expect/hope to be											

Figure 3. Analysis chart for in-depth exploration of your relationships. Copy out to avoid marking the book.

2: CONSTRUCTS

In the eight spaces provided along the top of the chart, write in eight constructs identified using the procedure described for Method One. Select four of the qualities which you ticked as desirable or attractive and four which you crossed as undesirable or unattractive. In the example opposite, Figure 4, Susan selected Happy; Clever; Popular and Amusing as her positive constructs and Cruel, Angry; Demanding and Lazy as negative constructs.

3: RANKING

Rank each person, from 1 to 8 according to the extent to which you feel he, or she, possesses that particular attribute.

Give rank (1) to the person you see as possessing that quality most strongly, working down to rank (8) for the individual to whom it is least applicable. Write down these rankings in each of the columns, starting at the left of the Chart and working to the right. Make sure that everybody gets a rank. If you wish to give people the same rank it is perfectly alright to do so, but you must then skip the next number. For instance if you give two subjects the rank of 3, then omit the 4 and rank the next person as 5.

As you can see in the example, Susan ranked her father as the happiest person she knew, and her mother as the second happiest. She ranked herself 'Now' at 3 and herself 'Later' at 4. Her best friend ranked 5 and someone she loved ranked 6. A person she disliked was ranked 7, and somebody she hated ranked 8.

4: CARRYING OUT THE ANALYSIS

Those familiar with statistics will see that I am describing a type of correlation known as Spearman's Rho. But you need not worry about why certain things are done in order to carry out the analysis perfectly accurately. Just follow the instructions carefully and check all your results.

(i) Taking any two columns of scores subtract the differences between each pair of ranks. Call this answer D, standing for 'difference'. In the example Susan started by taking the ranks for *Clever* away from the ranks for *Happy*. This produced the result shown below.

Construct Analysis Chart of Susan

People	Constructs							
	HAPPY	CLEVER	POPULAR	CRUEL	ANGRY	DEMANDING	LAZY	AMUSING
Somebody I love J.K.	6	6	8	8	7	8	1	3
Somebody I hate P.L.	8	7	1	1	8	2	8	8
Friend like being with B.D	5	2	7	7	6	7	2	2
Person dislike being with	7	8	2	2	2	1	7	7
My father	1	1	3	4	1	3	3	4
My mother	2	5	4	3	5	3	4	1
Me as I am now	3	3	6	5	4	5	6	6
Me I as expect/hope to be	4	4	5	6	3	6	5	5

Figure 4. A completed analysis chart in which each of the eight people have been ranked on the eight constructs, on ways of assessing others.

Happy	Clever	Difference (D) Between Ranks
6	6	0
8	7	1
5	2	3
7	8	−1
1	1	0
2	5	−3
3	3	0
4	4	0

As you see, where the rank for *Happy* was lower than the rank for *Clever* it produced a negative number.

To get rid of these negative numbers you now square each of the differences. Don't worry if you're a bit baffled about why squaring has this effect, simply multiply each number by itself.

Squaring the numbers in the example gives us the following:

Difference (D) Between Ranks	Different Squared
0	0
1	1
3	9
−1	1
0	0
−3	9
0	0
0	0

Next add up all the squared differences. In the example this gives us a total of 20 (1 + 9 + 1 + 9). We'll call this sum of the squares D^2

With this done you are ready to work out the correlation between the first two constructs using the formula given below.

$$\text{Correlation} = 1 - \frac{6 \times D^2}{504^*}$$

This means we must multiply the sum of the squares by 6, then divide the result by 504, which is why a calculator comes in handy. Finally we subtract the result from 1 to provide the correlation required.

For Susan this produced the following calculation:

---

* This number is based on a total of 8 people on the Chart. If you use more or less then recalculate this number using the formula $N(N^2 − 1)$ where N = the number of people on the Chart.

$$\text{Correlation between Happy and Clever} = 1 - \frac{6 \times 20}{504}$$

$$= 1 - \frac{120}{504}$$

$$= 1 - 0.24$$

$$= 0.76$$

As you can see the calculations are slightly tedious but not at all complicated. The result of Susan's analysis of these two construct showed a high, positive correlation which suggests that she sees the two as closely related.

She will expect happy people to be clever, and clever people to be happy. Just by looking at the way she ranked the chart we can get a very good sense of how various constructs are related to one another.

Now go back to the Chart, select two more constructs and repeat the whole procedure. For instance Susan might decide to be methodical and work out all the correlations between *Happy* and the remaining constructs:

> Happy – Popular.
> Happy – Cruel.
> Happy – Angry.
> Happy – Demanding.
> Happy – Lazy.
> Happy – Friendly.

That done she could start on Clever. Since the Happy–Clever correlation had already been calculated she would begin with: Clever – Popular, then go on to look at Clever – Cruel and so on.

You continue working with the chart until all the constructs have been correlated with one another.

Example of correlation table from analysis of a chart completed by Alison, a 33-year-old teacher.

184

	Kind	Stupid	Selfish	Sincere	Mean	Honest	Lazy	Dependable
Kind		−0.86	−0.69	0.78	−0.77	0.48	−0.56	0.95
Stupid	−0.86		0.86	−0.78	0.76	−0.10	0.95	−0.98
Selfish	−0.69	0.86		−0.95	0.62	−0.30	0.85	0.65
Sincere	0.78	−0.78	−0.95		−0.58	0.33	0.24	0.66
Mean	−0.77	0.76	0.62	−0.58		−0.66	0.75	−0.69
Honest	0.48	−0.10	−0.30	0.33	−0.66		−0.56	0.74
Lazy	−0.56	0.95	0.85	0.24	0.75	−0.56		−0.25
Dependable	0.95	−0.98	0.65	0.66	−0.69	0.74	−0.25	

You'll notice that the numbers above the diagonal are a mirror image of those below it. A moment's thought will make it clear why this must be the case. To make the task of interpreting the results easier, therefore, you can simplify it, without losing any information, if just one segment, either above or below the diagonal line, is left blank. When this is done you get the following:

	Kind	Stupid	Selfish	Sincere	Mean	Honest	Lazy
Kind							
Stupid	−0.86						
Selfish	−0.69	0.86					
Sincere	0.78	−0.78	−0.95				
Mean	−0.77	0.76	0.62	−0.58			
Honest	0.48	−0.10	−0.30	0.33	−0.66		
Lazy	−0.56	0.95	0.85	0.24	0.75	−0.56	
Dependable	0.95	−0.98	0.65	0.66	−0.69	0.74	−0.25

Even simplified in this way the chart looks fairly unapproachable and you shouldn't be surprised if, at first, you find it rather hard to pick out relationships. The best tactic is simple to take one of the constructs Alison has used, let's begin with *Kind* and see what this relates to. All the correlations are fairly high, suggesting significant relationships between this and the other constructs on the Chart. As we can see, Alison perceives kind people as not being stupid, selfish, lazy or mean (all high *negative* correlations), but as honest and dependable. This last relationship could be a clue to something quite significant in understanding her views of what makes a person attractive. If she rates kindness as an important and attractive quality, then she will tend to see this in terms of dependability. In other words when somebody lets her down she may like them a lot less because she now views them as not very kind.

Equally if she lets somebody down herself, this may lead to feelings of guilt because she could look on her lapse as proof that she was not a kindly person.

Interpreting these correlations is easier if we create a Mental Map as shown in the last chapter. Before explaining how this can be done, we should just consider how you use the methods described above to work out relationships between the people on the chart rather than the constructs.

All you have to do is reverse the order on the Chart, writing in people's initials across the top line, and placing constructs down the left-hand column where you previously wrote initials. Rank each person according to the quality you think they possess most and least.

When Susan did this for the first two people on the list, somebody she loved and somebody she hated, this was the result:

	Someone Loved	Someone Hated
Happy	3	8
Clever	5	2
Popular	2	7
Cruel	8	1
Angry	1	6
Demanding	4	3
Lazy	6	5
Warm	7	4

As one might expect there are marked differences between the people she loves and hates. By carrying out the analysis exactly as before the precise relationship between them can be calculated.

5: MAKING A MENTAL MAP

To illustrate the correlations in map form, as I demonstrated in chapter eight, you proceed as follows. Using the complete table, with both segments filled out, add up all the correlations in one column, while doing so IGNORE ALL MINUS SIGNS.

You may find this easier to do if you first remove the decimal point by multiplying each number by 100.

We'll return to Alison's correlation chart for an example of how to proceed after this addition is completed.

	Kind	Stupid	Selfish	Sincere	Mean	Honest	Lazy	Dependable
Kind		−86	−69	78	−77	48	56	95
Stupid	−86		86	−78	76	−10	95	−98
Selfish	−69	86		−95	62	−30	85	65
Sincere	78	−78	−95		−58	76	24	66
Mean	−77	76	62	−58		−66	75	−69
Honest	48	−10	−30	33	−66		−56	74
Lazy	56	95	85	24	75	−56		−25
Dependable	95	−98	65	66	−69	74	−25	
Total	509	529	492	432	483	317	416	492

These figures give us a measure of the important of each construct. The larger the total the greater the importance of that construct. Here the most significant one is that of Stupidity, with a score of 529 and the second most important that of being Kind with a total of 509.

Selecting the first construct to write down on the Mental Map is easy. We just pick the one with the highest total and write it down on the horizontal line of the chart.

Picking the second is a little trickier because we need to identify the construct with the highest score which also has the lowest correlation to the first construct.

Alison knew that Stupidity was her first construct, but dependable could not be the second because it correlated so highly with Stupidity (0.95). All the correlations are, in fact, very high with the lowest being found between Honesty and Stupidity at −0.10, and this was the one to write on the vertical line of the chart, as shown in the example opposite. The convention is always to write the first construct (with the highest total) on the horizontal line – technically called the abscissa – and the second construct on the vertical, or ordinate, line.

PLOTTING THE CONSTRUCTS

If you have ever looked up a street or town map, using the Index and reference co-ordinates provided, you will quickly get the hang of plotting constructs on the chart. Suppose, using the London AZ, I decided to look up Piccadilly Circus. The index provides me with a page number and the code 4C. This simply tells me to look for the letter C on the top of the page, and the number 4 down the side. Where lines projected from these two points meet I will find the Circus. All this is so straightforward that you may wonder why I repeat it here. It's simply because while most people find the task of locating places on a street map extremely easy they convince

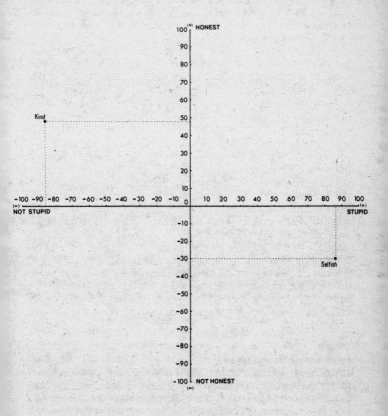

Figure 5. How the mental map is constructed.

themselves that the task of plotting a Mental Map is beyond them. Actually the two are very similar and equally simple.

All you have to do is select a construct and see how it relates to the two constructs identifying the horizontal and vertical lines on the chart, in the case of our example Stupidity and Honesty.

As the illustration shows, Figure 5, the top right section of the chart has all the positive values and the bottom left all the negative values. Top left has a mixture of positive and negative values, so too does the bottom right.

We'll start by plotting Kind. Looking at the table above we see that this is linked to Stupid by the number – 86. So we find this number on the horizontal line. Being a minus number it lies to the left of the vertical. Having found – 86, we next see how Kind relates to the second construct, Honest. This figure is 48. Being a positive number it will be found on the top part of the chart, as shown in the illustration. With these two figures we can locate Kind on our chart, mark it with a small cross and the word 'Kind'.

That done we turn our attention to the next construct, ignoring Stupid which is already on the chart, which is Selfish. This relates to Stupid at 86, and to Honest at – 30. The first number is positive and so locates the point to the right of the chart, the second being negative means we go below the below the horizontal line. As before the place where these co-ordinates meet locates the concept of Selfish on Alison's mental map.

The completed Mental Map, with all constructs plotted in the way described above, is shown opposite in Figure 6. What does this tell us about Alison's perceptions of people?

Immediately we can see that she regards honesty, kindness, sincerity and being dependable as all going together, and being related to not being stupid.

Equally, she sees being stupid as related to selfishness, being lazy mean, and not especially honest! All of which offers us some interesting insights into the way she sees others.

For a start the notion of stupidity, however she may define this, seems to play an important part in the way she views others. If she considers you stupid, you are also likely to find yourself construed as idle, selfish, mean and not very honest. If you are not seen as stupid, however, you'll be looked on as kind, sincere, dependable and honest. Tough luck, it seems, for any of her children who she begins to view as stupid!

The methods of analysis described here are, frankly, crude and do scant justice to Kelly's work but they take the subject as far as one reasonably can in a book intended for general readership. I hope too that they will offer you useful insights into your personal

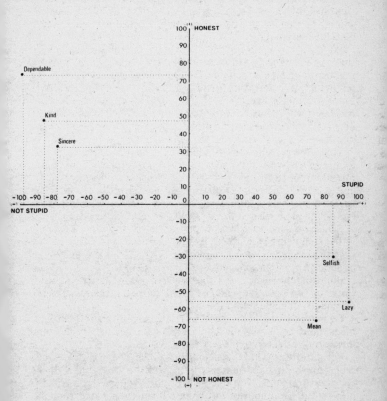

Figure 6. Alison's completed mental map, showing how some of the different ways in which she views other people relate together.

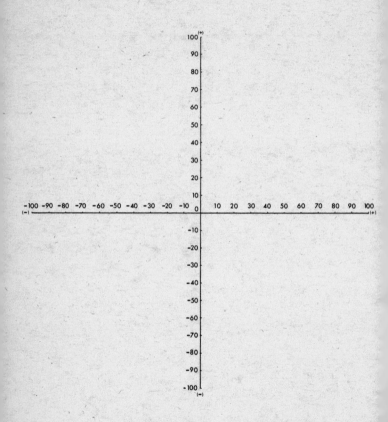

Figure 7. Copy out this grid if you would like to explore your own ways of viewing others.

construct system, although I caution against taking the results too
seriously. If you are interested in learning more of Kelly's theory
and methods for analysing grids then the reference section will
provide sources for further reading.

Bibliography

Adams-Webber, Jack *Personal Construct Theory*, Chichester: John Wiley and Sons, 1979.

Agnew, R., *Science Digest*, February 1984.

Allport, Gordon, *Personality*, London: Constable, 1971.

Ardrey, Robert, *The Social Contract*, New York: Atheneum, 1970.

Argyle, Michael, *Social Interaction*, London: Methuen & Co., 1969.

Asso, Doreen, *The Real Menstrual Cycle*, Chichester: John Wiley and Sons, 1983.

Baron, R. A., 'Olfaction and human social behaviour: effects of a pleasant scent on attraction and social perception', *Personality and Social Psychology Bulletin*, 7: 611–616, 1981.

Behan, Brendan, *Borstal Boy*, London: Hutchinson & Co., 1958.

Bell, Richard, and Harper, Lawrence, *Child Effects on Adults*, Hillsdale, New Jersey: Lawrence Erlbaum, 1977.

Bellak, Leopold, and Baker, Samm, *Reading Faces*, New York: Bantam Books, 1982.

Bender, N. P., 'Does construing people as similar involve similar behaviour towards them? A subjective and objective replication', *British Journal of Social and Clinical Psychology*, 15: 93–95, 1976.

Bensman, J., and Lilienfield, R., 'Friendship and Alienation', *Pyschology Today*, 56–66, 114, 1979.

Benton, D., 'Making sense of sex appeal', *The Guardian*, 10 July 1982.

Berger, E. M., 'The relation between expressed acceptance of self and expressed acceptance of others', *Journal Abnormal and Social Psychology*, 47: 778–782, 1952.

Berger, S. M., 'Conditioning through vicarious instigation', *Psychological Review*, 69, 450–466, 1962.

Bersheid, E., and Walster, E., 'Physical Attractiveness', *Advances in Experimental Social Psychology* 7, (ed. L. Berkowitz), New York: Academic Press, 1974.

Berscheid, E., and Walster, E., 'Beauty and the beast', *Psychology Today*, 74: 43–46, 1972.

Bettelheim, Bruno, *Surviving and Other Essays*, London: Thames and Hudson, 1979.

Bickman, L., 'The effects of social status on the honesty of others', *Journal of Social Psychology*, 85, 1971.

Bilgore, Ellen, 'Mammary Madness' *Omni Magazine*, 3, no. 9, July 1981.

Bloch, Ivan, *Sexual Life in England Past and Present*, London: Francis Aldor, 1938.

Bonarius, Han, Holland, Ray, and Rosenberg, Seymour, *Personal Construct Psychology*, London: Macmillan Publishers, 1981.

Brecher, Edward, *The Sex Researchers*, London: Andre Deutsch, 1970.

Bringle, R. G., and Williams, L. J., 'Parental offspring similarity on jealousy and related personality dimensions', *Motivation and Emotion*, 3: 265–285, 1979.

Brislin, R. W., and Lewis, S. A., 'Dating and physical attractiveness: replication', *Psychological Reports*, 22, 976, 1968.

Bronowski, J., and Mazlich, B., *The Western Intellectual Tradition*, London: Hutchinson, 1960.

Bryson, J. B., 'Situational determinants of the expression of jealousy': Paper presented at the 85th Annual Convention of the American Psychological Association, San Francisco, 1977.

Bull, Ray, 'The importance of being beautiful', *New Society*, p. 412, 14 November 1974.

Burns, R. B., *The Self-Concept*, London: Longman, 1979.

Byrne, Donn, *The Attraction Paradigm*, New York: Academic Press, 1971.

Byrne, Donn, and Baron, Robert, *Social Psychology: Understanding Human Interaction*, Boston: Allyn & Bacon Inc., 1974.

Casassus, Barbara, 'Saving face in job search', *Times Educational Supplement*, p. 18, 14 October 1983.

Cauthery, Philip, and Cole, Martin, *Fundamentals of Sex*, London: W. H. Allen, 1971.

Chandos, John, *Boys Together: English Public Schools 1800–1864*, London: Hutchinson, 1984.

Clarke, Anne, and Clarke, A. D. B., *Early Experience: Myth and Evidence*, London: Open Books, 1975.

Clifford, M. M., and Walster, E., 'Effect of physical attractiveness on teachers' expectations', *Sociology of Education*, 46: 248–258, 1973.

Cohen, R., *Patterns of Personality Judgement*, London: Academic Press, 1973.

194

Cook, Robin, *The Legacy of the Stiff Upper Lip*, London: Hutchinson, 1966.

Coward, R., *Female Desire*, London: Paladin, 1984.

Dawkins, Richard, *The Selfish Gene*, Oxford: Oxford University Press, 1976.

Deckert, Robert, 'Love formula', *Omni Magazine*, p. 49, June 1983.

De Mause, Lloyd (ed.), *The History of Childhood*, London: Souvenir Press, 1976.

Denzin, Norman, *On Understanding Emotion*, San Francisco: Jossey Bass, 1984.

Dinnerstein, Dorothy, *The Rocking of the Cradle: and the Ruling of the World*, London: Souvenir Press, 1976.

Dion, K. K., 'Physical attractiveness and evaluation of children's transgressions', *Journal of Personality and Social Psychology*, 24: 207–213, 1972.

Dion, K. K., Berscheid, E., and Walster, E., 'What is beautiful is good', *Journal of Personality and Social Psychology*, 24, 285–290, 1972.

Dollard, John, *Caste and Class in a Southern Town*, New Haven: Yale Press, 1937.

Doty, R. L., Huggins, G. R., Snyder, P. J., and Lowrey, L. D., 'Changes in the intensity and pleasantness of human vaginal odours during the menstrual cycle', *Science*, 190, 1316–1318, 1975.

Douty, H., 'The influence of clothing on the perception of persons', *Journal of Home Economics*, 55, 1963.

Down, J. L. H., 'Observations on ethnic classification of idiots', *London Hospital Reports*, pp. 259–262, 1866.

Ellis, Havelock, *Man and Woman*, New York: Charles Scribner, 1894.

Ellis, Havelock, *The Criminal*, New York: Charles Scribner, 1910.

Ellis, Gary, 'Pavlovian Sex', *Science*, p. 72, May 1984.

Engen, T., 'Why the aroma lingers on', *Psychology Today*, 138, May 1980.

Erickson, Erik, *Identity: Youth and Crisis*, London: Faber & Faber, 1968.

Eysenck, Hans, *The Measurement of Personality*, Lancaster: MTP Press, 1976.

Filsinger, E. E., and Anderson, C. C., 'Social class and self-esteem in late adolescence: dissonant context or self-efficacy', *Developmental Psychology*, 18: 380–384, 1982.

Frankel, S., and Sherick, I., 'Observations on the development of normal envy', *Formal Studies of the Child*, 32: 257–281, 1977.

Friedrich, Otto, *Before The Deluge*, New York: Harper and Row, 1972.

Fromm, Erich, *The Fear of Freedom*, London: Routledge & Kegan Paul, 1960.

Fryer, Peter, (ed.), *The Man of Pleasures Companion*, London: Arthur Barker, 1968.

Galton, Francis, *Memories of My Life*, London: Methuen, 1909.

Gagnon, J., and Simon W., 'On psycho-sexual development', *Handbook of Research and Theory in Socialisation*, ed. D. Goslin, New York: Rand, 1969.

Gauld, Alan, and Shotter, John, *Human Action and its Psychological Investigation*, London: Routledge & Kegan Paul, 1977.

Goffman, Ervin, *Presentation of Self in Everyday Life*, New York: Doubleday, 1959.

Goffman, Ervin, *Asylums*, New York: Doubleday, 1961.

Goffman, Ervin, *Relations in Public: Microstudies of the Public Order*, London: Allen Lane, The Penguin Press, 1971.

Gould, Stephen Jay, *The Mismeasure of Man*, New York: W. W. Norton, 1971.

Griffitt, W., and Veitch, R., 'Fall-out shelter. Hot and crowded. Influence of population density and temperature on interpersonal affective behaviour', *Journal of Personality and Social Psychology*, 17: 92–98, 1971.

Griffitt, W., and Veitch R., 'Preacquaintance attitude similarity and attraction revisited: Ten days in a fall-out shelter', *Sociometry*, 37, 163–173, 1974.

Hamachek, D. E., *Encounters with the Self*, New York: Holt Reinhart and Winston, 1978.

Hamid, P. N., 'Some effects of dress curs on observational accuracy, perceptual estimate, and impression formation', *Journal of Social Psychology*, 86, 1972.

Hammond, W. H., 'The Status of Physical Types', *Human Biology*, 29: 233–241, 1957.

Harlow, H. F., *Learning to Love*, San Francisco: Albion, 1971.

Harlow, H. F., and Harlow M. K., 'Learning to Love', *American Scientist*, 54: 244–272, 1966.

Harris, Anthony, 'A simple way to classify physique', *General Practitioner*, pp. 24–25, June 4 1976.

Harris, Thomas, *I'm OK – You're OK*, New York: Harper and Row, 1967.

Henriques, Fernando, *Love In Action*, London: MacGibbon and Keen, 1959.

Henriques, Fernando, *Prostitution in Europe and the New World*, 2, London: Macgibbon & Kee, 1963.

Hess, E. H., and Polt, J. M., 'Pupil size as related to the interest value of visual stimuli', *Science*, 132: 349–350, 1960.

Hinde, Robert, *Non-Verbal Communication*, Cambridge: Cambridge University Press, 1972.

Hitler, Adolf, *Mein Kampf*, translated by Ralph Manheim, London: Hutchinson, 1974.

Hochberg, J., and Galper, R. E., 'Attribution of intention as a function of physiognomy', *Memory and Cognition*. 2: 39–42, 1974.

Horney, K., *Neurosis and Human Growth*, New York: W. W. Norton, 1950.

Hovland, Carl, and Sears, Robert, 'Minor studies of aggression: Correlation of lynching with economic factors', *Journal of Psychology*, 9: 301–310, 1940.

Hudson, J. W., and Henze L. F., 'Campus values in mate selection: a replication', *Journal of Marriage and the Family*, 31: 772–775, 1969.

Humphreys, L. G., 'Characteristics of type concepts with special reference to Sheldon's typology', *Psychological Bulletin*, 54: 218–228, 1957.

Hurlock, Elizabeth, *Adolescent Development*, New York: McGraw Hill, 1955.

Izard, C. E., 'Personality similarity and friendship', *Journal Abnormal Social Psychology*, 67: 404–408, 1960.

James, William, *Principles of Psychology*, New York: Holt, 1890.

Jerslid, J., *Boy Prostitution*, Copenhagen: G.E.C. Gad, 1956.

Johnson, M. P., and Leslie, L., 'Couple involvement and network structure, a test of the dyadic withdrawal hypotheses', *Social Psychology Quarterly*, 45: 39–43, 1982.

Kalven, Harry, and Zeisel, Hans, *The American Jury*, Chicago: Chicago University Press, 1966.

Karlen, Arno, *Sexuality and Homosexuality*, London: Macdonald, 1971.

Karlins, M., Coffman, T. L., and Walter, G., 'On the fading of social stereotypes: studies in three generations of college students', *Journal of Personality and Social Psychology*, 13: 1–16, 1969.

Kellog, W. N., and Kellog, L. A., *The Ape and the Child*, London: McGraw Hill, 1933.

Kelly, George, *The Psychology of Personal Constructs*, New York: W. W. Norton, 1955.

Kernis, M. H., and Wheeler, L., 'Beautiful friends and ugly strangers: radiation and contrast effects in perceptions of same-sex pairs', *Personality and Social Psychology Bulletin*, 7: 617–620, 1981.

Keverne, E. B., 'Pheromones' in Nicholson, J., and Foss, B., (eds), *Psychological Survey*, 4, Leicester: BPS.

Kiefer, Otto, *Sexual Life in Ancient Rome*, London: The Abbey Library, 1934.

Kinsey, A., et al., *Sexual Behaviour in the Human Female*, Philadelphia: W. B. Saunders Co., 1953.

Knapp, M. L., *Nonverbal Communication in Human Interaction*, New York: Holt Reinhart & Winston, 1972.

Knight, Stephen, *The Brotherhood*, London: Granada, 1983.

Kohler, W., *The Mentality of Apes*, London: Routledge & Kegan Paul, Trench, Turner & Co.

Kraft-Ebbing, Richard, *Psychopathia Sexualis*, New York: G. P. Putnam & Sons, 1965.

Kretschmer, E., *Physique and Character*, (2nd edition), translated by W. J. H. Spratt, New York: Harcourt Brace & World Inc., 1925.

Krich, Aron (ed.), *The Sexual Revolution: Seminal Studies into 20th Century American Sexual Behaviour*, 2, New York: Dell Publishing, 1965.

Lamb, Warren and Watson, Elizabeth, *Body Code*, London: Routledge & Kegan Paul, 1979.

Lea, M., 'Personality similarity in unreciprocated friendships', *British Journal of Social and Clinical Psychology*, 18: 393–394, 1979.

Lefkowitz, M., Blake, R., and Mouton, J., 'Status factors in pedestrian violation of traffic signals', *Journal of Abnormal and Social Psychology*, 51, 1955.

Levinger, G., 'A three-level approach to attraction: toward an understanding of pair-relatedness', in *Foundations of Interpersonal Attraction*, ed. T. L. Houston, New York: Academic Press, 1974.

Levinger, G., and Breedlove, J., 'Interpersonal attraction and agreement: a study of marriage partners', *Journal of Personality and Social Psychology*, 3: 367–372, 1969.

Lewis, David, *The Secret Language of Your Child*, London: Souvenir Press, 1978.

Lewis, David, and Hughman, Peter, *Just How Just*, London: Secker and Warburg, 1975.

Licht, Hans, *Sexual Life In Ancient Greece*, London: The Abbey Library, 1932.

Lickona, Thomas, *Moral Development and Behaviour*, New York: Holt Reinhart and Winston, 1976.

198

Liebowitz, Michael R., *The Chemistry of Love*, New York: Little Brown, 1983.

Light, L., Hollander, H., and Kayra-Stuart, *Personality and Social Psychology Bulletin*, 7: 209.

Lindzey, Gardner, and Aronson, Elliot, *The Handbook of Social Psychology*, 3, Reading, Massachusetts: Addison-Wesley, 1969.

Lipsett, L. P., Engen T., and Kaye, H., 'Developmental changes in the olfactory threshold of the neonate', *Child Development*, 34: 371–376, 1963.

Llewellyn-Jones, Derek, *Human Reproduction & Society*, London: Faber & Faber, 1973.

Lombroso, C., *Crime: its causes and remedies*, Boston: Little Brown, 1911.

Lombroso, C., *L'Homme criminel*, Paris: F. Alcan, 1887.

Lombroso, C., 'Criminal anthropology applied to pedagogy', *Monist* 6: 50–59, 1895.

Lombroso, C., *The Female Offender*, London: Peter Owen, 1958.

Lorenz, Konrad, *On Aggression*, New York: Harcourt Brace and World Inc., 1966.

Lorenz, K. Z., *The Foundations of Ethology*, New York: Springer Verlag.

Macfarlane, A., 'Olfaction in the development of social preferences in the human neonate', *Ciba Symposium: Parent–infant interaction*, 33: 103–113, 1975.

Mancuso, James C., and Adams-Webber, Jack, *The Construing Person*, New York: Praeger, 1982.

Marcus, Steven, *The Other Victorians*, London: Weidenfeld and Nicolson, 1964.

Milgram, Stanley, *Obedience to Authority*, London: Tavistock Publications, 1974.

Miller, A., 'Role of physical attractiveness in impression formation', *Psychonomic Science*, 4, 1970.

Miller, Neal and Bugelski, Richard, 'Minor studies in aggression: The influence of frustrations imposed by the in-group on attitudes expressed toward out-groups', *Journal of Psychology*, 25: 437–442, 1948.

Milne, Hugo, and Hardy, Shirley, *Psycho-Sexual Problems*, Bradford: Bradford University Press, 1976.

Money, J., and Ehrhardt, A., *Man and Woman Boy and Girl*, Baltimore: John Hopkins University Press.

Montague, Ashley, *Touching*, New York: Harper and Row, 1977.

Morris, Desmond, *The Naked Ape*, London: Jonathan Cape, 1967.

Morris, Desmond, Collett, Peter, Marsh, Peter, and

O'Shaughnessy, Marie, *Gestures – Their Origin & Distribution*, London: Jonathan Cape, 1979.

Morris, N. M., and Udry, J. R., 'Study of the relationship between coitus and LH surge', *Fertility and Sterility*, 28: 440–442, 1977.

Muller, J., *De Febre Amatoria*, London, 1689.

Newcomb, T. M., *The acquaintance process*, New York: Holt Reinhart & Winston, 1961.

Murstein, B. I., (ed.), *Theories of Attraction and Love*, New York: Springer, 1970.

Newcomb, T. M., 'Dyadic balance as a source of clues about interpersonal attraction', *Theories of Attraction and Love*, ed. B. I. Murstein, New York: Springer, 1971 (op. cit.).

Nicolaides, J., 'Skin lipids: their biochemical uniqueness', *Science* 186: 19–24, 1974.

Oakley, Ann, *Sex Gender and Society*, London: Temple Smith, 1972.

Oatley, Keith, *Selves in Relation*, London: Methuen, 1984.

Packard, Vance, *The Sexual Revolution*, London: Longmans, 1968.

Parlee, M. B., and *Psychology Today* editors, 'The friendship bond', *Psychology Today*, 45–45, October 1979.

Partridge, Burco, *A History of Orgies*, London: Spring Books, 1958.

Pearsall, Ronald, *The Worm in the Bud: The World of Victorian Sexuality*, London: Weidenfeld and Nicolson, 1969.

Peele, Stanton, *Love and Addiction*, London: Abacus, 1977.

Ratcliffe, Rosemary (ed.), *Dear Worried Brown Eyes: Letters and replies from women's magazines over three centuries*, London: Pergamon Press, 1969.

Perrin, F. A. C., 'Physical attractiveness and repulsiveness', *Journal of Experimental Psychology*, 4: 203–207, 1921.

Remarque, Erich Maria, *All Quiet On The Western Front*, translated by A. W. Wheen, London: G. P. Putnam's Sons, 1929.

Richey, M. H., and Richey, H. W., 'The significance of best-friend relationships in adolescence', *Psychology in the Schools*, 17: 536–540, 1980.

Rist, R. C., 'Student social class and teacher expectations: the self-fulfilling prophecy in ghetto education', *Harvard Educational Review*, 40: 411–451, 1970.

Roberts, Stephen, *The House That Hitler Built*, London: Methuen, 1937.

Rossman, Parker, *Sexual Experiences Between Men and Boys*, London: Maurice Temple Smith, 1979.

Rugoff, Milton, *Prudery and Passion: Sexuality in Victorian America*, London: Hart Davis, 1971.

200

Russel, M. J., 'Human olfactory communication', *Nature*, 13: 737–739, 1980.

Russell, M. J., Switz, G. M., and Thompson, K., 'Olfactory influences on the human menstrual cycle', *Pharmacology Biochemistry and Behaviour*, 13: 737–738, 1980.

Sachs, Oliver, *Awakenings*, London: Duckworth 1973.

Salvo Vincent, Di, *Business and Professional Communication*, Columbus, Ohio: Charles E. Merrill Publishing Company, 1977.

Schaffer, H. R., *Studies in Mother–Infant Interaction*, London: Academic Press, 1977.

Schofield, Michael, *The Sexual Behaviour of Young People*, London: Longmans, 1965.

Schonemann, P., Byrne, D., and Bell, P. A., 'A statistical reinterpretation of an attraction model', unpublished manuscript, Purdue University, 1976.

Schur, Edwin (ed.), *The Family and the Sexual Revolution*, London: George Allen and Unwin, 1964.

Schofield, W., *Psychotherapy: The Purchase of Friendship*, Englewood Cliffs, New Jersey: Prentice-Hall, 1964.

Selman, R. L., and Selman, A. P., 'Children's ideas about friendship: a new theory', *Psychology Today*, 71–80, 114, October 1979.

Seymour-Smith, Martin, *Fallen Women*, London: Thomas Nelson, 1969.

Shaw, Mildred, *Recent Advances in Personal Construct Technology*, London: Academic Press, 1981.

Sheldon, William, *Atlas of Men: A Guide for Somatyping the Adult Male at all Ages*, New York: Harper and Row, 1954.

Sheldon, W. H., Stevens, S. S., and Tucker, W. B., *The Varieties of Human Physique*, New York: Harper and Row, 1940.

Shepherd Eric and Watson, J. P., *Personal Meanings*, Chichester: John Wiley and Sons, 1982.

Sherif, Muzafer, *Group Conflict & Co-operation*, London: Routledge & Kegan Paul, 1967.

Shorter, Edward, *The Making of The Modern Family*, London: Collins, 1976.

Sigal, H., and Ostrove, N., 'Effects of the physical attractiveness of the defendant and nature of crime on juridic judgement', Paper presented at the 81st Annual Convention of the American Psychological Society.

Slater, Patrick (ed.), *Explorations of Intrapersonal Space*, Chichester: John Wiley and Sons, 1979.

Solomon, Robert, *The Passions*, New York: Doubleday, 1976.

Storr, Anthony, *Human Aggression*, London: Allen Lane, The Penguin Press, 1968.

Tesser, A., and Brodie, M., 'A note on the evaluation of a computer date', *Psychonomic Science*, 23: 300, 1971.

Tipton, R. M., and Benedictson, C. S., Maloney, J., and Hartnett, J. J., 'Development of a scale for assessment of jealousy', *Psychological Reports*, 42: 1217–1218, 1978.

Tyler, Leona, *The Psychology of Human Differences*, Englewood Cliffs, New Jersey; Prentice Hall, 1965.

Walker, R. N., 'Body build and behaviour in your children: II body build and parents ratings', *Child Development*, 34: 1–23, 1963.

Walster, E., Aronson, E., and Abrahams, D., 'On increasing the persuasiveness of a low prestige communicator', *Journal of Personality and Social Psychology*, 4: 508–516, 1966.

Walster, E., Aronson, E., Abrahams D., and Rottman, L., 'Importance of physical attractiveness in dating behaviour', *Journal of Personality and Social Psychology*, 4: 508–516, 1966.

Weatherly, Donald, 'Ant-Semitism and the expression of fantasy aggression', *Journal of Abnormal and Social Psychology*, 62: 454–457, 1961.

Wedeck, H. E., *Dictionary of Aphrodisiacs*, London: Peter Owen, 1964.

West, D. J., *Homosexuality*, London: Penguin Books, 1955.

White, G. L., 'A model of romantic jealousy', *Motivation and Emotion*, 5: 295–310, 1981.

Wiggins, J. S., Wiggins, N., and Conger, J. C., 'Correlates of heterosexual somatic preference', *Journal of Personality and Social Psychology*, 10: 82–90, 1968.

Wilder, Rachel, 'Love Signals', *Science Digest*, June 1984.

Wilson, G., and Nias, D., *The Mystery of Love: The Hows and Whys of Sexual Attraction*, New York: Quadrangle, 1976.

Winch, R. F., *The Modern Family*, New York: Holt, Reinhart and Winston, 1952.

Wunderlich, Paul, 'Hooked on Love', *Omni Magazine*, August 1984.

Zion, L. C., 'Body concept as it relates to self-concept', *Research Quarterly*, 36: 490–495, 1965.

Zunin, Leonard, and Zunin, Natalie, *Contact: the First Four Minutes*, New York: Ballantine Books, 1972.

Index